15/-

SREEMAD BHAGAWAD GEETA

CHAPTER VI

ORIGINAL SANSKRIT TEXT WITH
ROMAN TRANSLITERATION, WORD-FOR-WORD MEANING.
TRANSLATION AND COMMENTARY

BY

SWAMI CHINMAYANANDA

Central Chinmaya Mission Trust
Mumbai - 400 072

Edition		1983 -	5,000 copies
Reprint		1991 -	3,000 copies
Reprint		1993 -	3,000 copies
Reprint	November	2001 -	2,000 copies
Reprint	July	2003 -	1,000 copies

Published by :
Central Chinmaya Mission Trust
Sandeepany Sadhanalaya
Saki Vihar Road, Mumbai - 400 072. India.
Tel. : 091-22-2857 2367, 2857 5806
Fax : 091-22-2857 3065
Email : ccmt@vsnl.com
Website : www.chinmayamission.com

Distribution Centre in USA :
Chinmaya Mission West
Publications Division
560 Bridgetown Pike,
Langhorne, PA 19053, USA
Tel.: (215)396-0390 Fax: (215)396-9710
www.chinmayapublications.org
publications@chinmaya.org

Printed by :
Priya Graphics
J-120, Ansa Industrial Estate,
Saki Vihar Road, Sakinaka,
Mumbai - 400 072.
Tel.: 5695 99 35 Telefax : 2852 80 97
Email : chinmayapriya@roltanet.com

Price : Rs. 15.00

ISBN : 81-7597-088-X

GEETA
CHAPTER SIX

INTRODUCTION

WITH this chapter we are coming to the close of a definite section in the scheme of thought in the Geeta: this is the opinion of some of the well-known critics and students of the Lord's Song. According to them, the entire eighteen chapters of the Geeta can fall into three definite sections, each of six chapters, and they group themselves to expound the implications and significances of the sacred Vedic mantra *Tat tvam asi*— 'That thou art.' The first six chapters together constitute, in their contents and explanation, the philosophical significance indicated by the word 'Thou' *(tvam).* In the general scheme of thought developed in that section, the contents of chapter six constitute a fitting conclusion.

In Chapter II, in a language almost foreign to Arjuna, in quick strokes, Lord Krishna painted the philosophical perfection which is the theme of all the Upanishads. He concluded that chapter with a vivid and expressive picture of a saint of perfection and mental equipoise. Naturally, the interest of a seeker is excited, and he seeks to find means and methods by which he too can grow within himself into those divine heights of self-control and equipoise.

The Geeta is personally and specifically addressed to Arjuna, a confused average man, at a moment when he felt completely confounded by the problem that was facing him. Naturally, the highest methods of subtle meditation, of the mental drill by which each can renounce all his preoccupations, etc., are not easy methods which can be practised with confidence. At the same time, it will not be true to say that Vedantic methods are meant only for a few; if it is immediately useful only to the few, there must be in Vedanta preliminary techniques by which everyone can steadily grow to become fit to enter the Hall of Perfection.

That there are graded lessons for the spiritual unfoldment, is not really understood by the modern lip-Vedantins. It is this general ignorance that has brought the misconception in Hinduism that the study of the Vedas is the guarded preserve of some rare ones. And Vedanta would have been an incomplete science if it did not contain *upasana* methods for purifying the students' inner equipments.

Krishna, as a true teacher, understood Arjuna's mental debility and intellectual incompetency at that particular moment to start right away the arduous lines of pure meditation and clear, detached thinking. In order to bring him to the level of perfection, various lower methods of self-integration were to be prescribed in the treatment of Arjuna. Thus in Chapter III we found an exhaustively scientific treatment of the *Karma-Yoga*—the Path of Action.

Activities in the outer world, however noble they may be in their motive, cannot but leave deep ulcerations and painful restlessness in the bosom of the worker. To mitigate the 'reactions' of actions. *(karma-phalam),* as a balm to soothen the bleeding mental wounds, new methods of maintaining the mind in quietude and ease had been expounded in Chapter IV under the title *'Renunciation of Action in Knowledge'.* By constantly maintaining in the mind the awareness of the greater principle that presides over all human endeavours, it is the theory of Krishna that the worker can, even in the thick of activities, maintain a healthy and well-ventilated inner life.

Naturally, the limited intellect of Arjuna got extremly confused since his teacher argued in the beginning for 'action', and in the conclusion for 'renunciation of action'. In Chapter V, therefore, the '*Way of Renunciation'* is explained, and the technique of guaranteeing immunity to our mind from reactions even while it is engaged in activity is explained. The '*yagna*-spirit' —the spirit of self-dedicated activity for the benefit of the larger majority and not for any self-arrogating profit—is the antiseptic that Krishna prescribes for a mind and intellect that are to work in the world. In chapter IV, an unavoidable treatment is prescribed for the mind for curing its own pox of painful 'impressions of the past' (*vasanas).*

In Chapter V. the *Way of Renunciation* is explained under two different categories, which show the two methods of achieving the same goal: Renunciation of (a) our sense of agency in activities, and (b) our unintelligent anxieties arising out of our thoughtless preoccupations with the fruits of our action. The chapter exhausts these two techniques and explains how, by the renunciation of our attachment to the fruits of action we can come to gain a release from the *vasana*-bondages which generally shackle our personality during our activities.

One who can faithfully follow the technique so far unravelled by the Lord should have, thereby, come to a condition wherein the insentient and inert mind has been stirred into a field of intense activity. A mind developed through the training is taught to come under the intelligent will of its determined trainer, the very seeker. The mind thus gathered and trained is certainly a better equipped instrument for the higher purpose of Self-contemplation and Self-unfoldment.

How this is done through the famous technique of meditation is, in a nutshell, the theme of the sixth chapter. During our discussions we shall not stand in sheer surprise and wonderment and swallow down the ideas in the verses without dissecting, discovering, analysing, and understanding every facet of each of the ideas. This chapter promises to give us all the means by which we can give up our own known weaknesses and positively grow into a healthier and more potent life of virtue and strength. This technique is called meditation which, in one form or the other, is the common method advocated and advised in all religions by all prophets at all times. in the history of man.

अथ षष्ठोऽध्याय:

श्रीभगवानुवाच

अनाश्रित: कर्मफलं कार्यं कर्म करोति य: ।
स संन्यासी च योगी च न निरग्निर्न चाक्रिय: ॥

Srī. Bhagavān uvāca
1. anāśritaḥ karmaphalam
kāryam karma karotiyaḥ
sa samnyāsī ca yogī ca
na niragnir na cākriyaḥ

अनाश्रित:- not depending (on) कर्मफलम् - fruit of action, कार्यम् - bounden, कर्म - duty, करोति - performs, य:- who, स:- he, संन्यासी - Sannyasi (ascetic) च - and, योगी - Yogi च - and, न - not, निरग्नि:- without fire, न - not च - and, अक्रिय:- without action.

The Blessed Lord said:

1. He who performs his bounden duty without depending on the fruits of action-he is a *sannyasin* and a *Yogin;* not he who (has renounced) is without fire and without action.

Apart from what we said in the Introduction, another school of thought classifies the Geeta and attributes the first six chapters to what is called *Karma-kanda* in the Vedas. According to them, the second bulk of six chapters in the Geeta constitutes the *Upasanakanda,* and the last team of six chapters represents the *Gyanakanda* of the Vedas. Accepting this classification for the time being, we can appreciate Sree Sankara's insistence that this opening stanza of the chapter is a glorification of the householder who pursues his life of ritualism in a spirit of service and dedication unto the Lord.

To accept the view that Krishna is here advocating or glorifying the life of ritualism, would be a contradiction to the background against which the Geeta has been so laboriously woven out. In the Lord's Song. Krishna is advising Arjuna—a misinformed prince who was trying to behave against his own culture. The warrior is now standing in the battlefront, wanting to run away, and Krishna, his friend and charioteer, is trying to persuade the Pandava prince to stick to his bow and arrow. At this juncture, to assume that the Lord is glorifying 'God-dedicated performance of domestic ritualism', would be a miserable contradiction.

Directly read, the stanza clearly gives its simple meaning. and no annotation seems necessary. Without much coaxing, the Verse readily smiles forth its meaning to any clear thinking reader. So far we have been discussing, in the previous chapters, two parallel ideas running a neck-to-neck race for importance, namely, 'renunciation of the sense of agency' (*sannyasa)* and the 'renunciation of attachment to the fruits of action' *(Yoga)*. Naturally, in this chapter, in the very opening stanza, Bhagavan had to indicate that the '*sannyasi* is himself the '*Yogi'*, and that seekers must, therefore, tirelessly employ themselves in noble endeavours, renouncing both their sense of agency and their anxiety for the fruits of action.

Arjuna's plan, in his own words in the first chapter, was to escape the battlefield in order to live the *sannyasa*-life. He did not know that a true Yogi (selfless worker) is himself the greatest *sannyasi,* for, without renunciation, his action would become at best only a mischievous meddling with the harmony of the universe.

As a revivalist of Hinduism, Vyasa cannot stop with merely putting this idea into the mouth of Lord Krishna. The missionary zeal with which the Geeta has been expounded demands a direct hit on the existing misunderstanding in the days of Arjuna regarding true renunciation. In the Mahabharata time, *sannyasa* has come to symbolise crudely a formal exterior without the soft perfections within. Mere external symbolism has come to mark *sannyasa* without it, accompaniments of mental purity and intellectual equipoise, which must ever be the real badges of a true renouncer. Arjuna had a feeling that *sannyasa* meant renunciation of activities, symbolised here in the language of those days as fire, and, thereafter, living without any duty or work.

To escape from the buzzle of life, in our present state of unpreparedness, into the quiet atmosphere of the banks of the Ganges is only a fall of an averge good man to the level of the insentient stone in the very Ganges. At the close of this verse, Krishna laughs at Arjuna's sad misconceptions. There is no bitterness in the irony of the Lord. Soon we shall find that Arjuna also comes to laugh at his own misunderstandings.

The whole chapter is so fully and entirely dedicated to expounding the technique of cultivation, direction, and application of the inner forces of thoughts and feelings that it is very appropriate for Krishna to indicate the greater importance of revolutionising our inner motives and mental attitudes before we enter the path of spirituality.

As an elucidting annotation for the quibble whih the Lord had declared in this stanza, we have His added explanations in the following which shows how sannyasa itself is Yoga :

यं संन्यासमिति प्राहुर्योगं तं विद्धि पाण्डव ।
न ह्यसंन्यस्तसंकल्पो योगी भवति कश्चन ॥ २ ॥

2. *yam samnyāsm iti prāhur*
yogam tam viddhi pāṇḍava
na hy asamnyasta-samkalpo
yogī bhavati kaścana

यम् - which, संन्यासम् - renunication, इति -thus, प्राहुः- (they) call, योगम् - Yoga, तम् - that, विद्धि - know, पाण्डव - O Pandava, न - not, हि - verily, असंन्यस्तसंकल्पः- one who has not renounced thoughts, योगी-Yogi, भवति - becomes, कश्चन - anyone.

2. O Pandava, please know Yoga to be that which they call renuciation; no one verily becomes a Yogi who has not renounced thoughts.

Lord Krishna is repeating the same idea lest Arjuna should overlook the fact that what they call as *sannyasa,* the 'renunciation of agency'. is itself *Yoga,* the 'renunciation of the fruits-of-action'. *Sannyasa* is the state reached through *Yoga,* the practice; and the spiritual practice of *Yoga* cannot even be thought of without the spirit of *sannyasa* in the bosom: One is the obverse and the other the reverse of the same coin of spiritual perfection.

It is but natural that the intellectually independent thinker in Arjuna should, at this juncture, ask the question 'why?' with his raised brows. Seeing this, the Charioteer implicitly gives the logical reasons behind his seemingly outrageous and daring conclusion. The Lord explains that never can one become established in the practices of one's own cultural rehabilitation unless one learns the art of renouncing all *sankalpas.*

Unfortunately, the term *sankalpa* cannot be translated in the language in which we are now talking. Language is a medium of expression discovered by people to exchange their ideas and ideologies. The Englishman has not yet penetrated deeper than his flesh into his scientific study of life, and, therefore, the term, *sankalpa,* which belongs to the world of the mind and intellect, has not yet been crystallized by this language into any familiar, single soundsymbol. However, we can try to give our readers a hazy notion of what all constitute the term *sankalpa.*

Man cannot remain ordinarily without imagining and constantly creating in his exuberant fancy. And, in his imagination, he invariably tries to pull down the beautiful veil thrown over the face of the future. Ripping open this veil over the Unknown, everyone of us, on all occasions in our imaginations, fix for ourselves a goal to be fulfilled by us in the near future. Having fixed up the temporary goal, our mind plans and creates a method of achieving that hazy goal. But ere we execute our plans and enter into the field of effort to carve out success for ourselves, the never-tiring and ever-active power of imagination in us would have already wiped clean the earlier-fixed goal for achievement and rewritten a modified destination to be gained in the future.

Again, by the time we prepare ourselves mentally and start executing our ideas in our life, our mischievous fancy would have already wiped clean the distant goal. Thus, each time the goal remains only so long as we have not started our pilgrimage to it; and the moment we start the pilgrimage, the goal fades away from our vision!

In short, when we have got a goal, we have not started acting, and the moment we start the strife, we seem to have no goal to reach. The subtle force in our inner composition, which unconsciously creates this lunatic temperament in us, is called the unbridled *sankalpa sakti.*

We need no help from any great commentators to understand that no achievement, either without or within us, can be gained so long as we have not pursued, arrested, and finally destroyed this dangerous inner saboteur called *sankalpa*. To show that there is no compromise in this, Bhagavan is using a very positive term that none (*kaschana)* can ever reach any progress on the path of self-redemption without acquiring for oneself a capacity to renounce this self-poisoning *sankalpha*-disturbances.

'Karma Yoga, practised without regard to the fruit of action, forms an external aid (bahiranga sadhana) to Dhyana Yoga. The Lord now proceeds to show how Karma-Yoga is a means to better and greater meditation.'

आरुरुक्षोर्मुनेर्योगं कर्म कारणमुच्यते ।
योगारूढस्य तस्यैव शमः कारणमुच्यते ॥ ३ ॥

3. āruruksor muner yogam
karma kāraṇam ucyate
yogārūḍhasya tasyaiva
śamaḥ kāraṇam ucyate

आरुरुक्षोः - wishing to climb, मुनेः - of a Muni or sage, योगम् - Yoga, कर्म - action, कारणम् - the cause, उच्यते - is said, योगारूढस्य - of one who has attained (to Yoga), तस्य - of him, एव - even, शम - inaction (quiescence), कारणम् - the cause, उच्यते - is said.

3. For a *muni* or sage who 'wishes to attain to *Yoga*', action is said to be the means; for the same sage who has 'attained to *Yoga*', inaction (quiescence) is said to be the means.

To one who is '*desiring to scale over the practice of mental concentration and self-improvement, work is said to be the means.*' By working in the world with neither the egocentric concept of agency nor the egocentric desires for the fruits of those actions, we are creating within ourselves a convenient atmosphere for the existing *vasanas* to play out without creating any new precipitate of fresh impression.*

The metaphor used here is borrowed from riding, and is very powerful in its suggestions. Before we ride over a steed which is wild, to some extent it drives you, rather than the other way. For one who desires to bring a steed under his own perfect control, there is a period when, with one leg on the stirrup, the individual has to hang on to the saddle and, with the other leg on the ground, learn to kick himself off from the ground and spring up to throw his legs over the back of the animal, until he sits with the steed completely between his own legs. Having mounted, it is easy to control the animal; but, till then, the rider, in his attempt to mount the horse, must pass through a stage where he is neither totally on the horse nor on the ground.

In the beginning we are merely workers in the world—desire-prompted and ego-driven we sweat and toil, weep and sob. When an individual gets tired of such activities, he comes to desire to mount the steed of his mind. Such an individual, desiring to bring the mind under his control and ride over it *(aruruksha)*, takes upon himself the same work as before, but without the ego and his ego-centric desires. Such desireless activities, undertaken in the *Yagna* spirit explained earlier,** cleanse the mind of its past impressions and intergrate the entire inner equipment. When thus the required amount of concentration has been gained by the individual as a result of the *vasana*-purgation effected, he is to stop his activities slowly and apply himself more and more to live in deeper meditation. When once his mind has been conquered and his agitations

---

* *See 'General Introduction, Chapter. I.*

** *Chapter IV, Stanzas 18-21, and 25-30.*

have become well controlled, the seeker in that state of mental growth and development is termed as 'having mounted the steed of the mind'. (*Yoga-arudha).* To such an individual, at that state of his mental equipoise and self-application, 'quiescence' (*sama)* is the means for gaining a higher perfection and self-growth.

By thus describing two means at the two distinct stages of the individual's growth, it is meant that they are not contradictory. Selfless activity is good at a stage,but, afterwards, it becomes a positive agitation which brings the mind down from its serener flights to bump frequently on the ground with a shattering shock. Specially prepared milk powder, diluted with hot water, is the full diet for an infant. But the same feeding-bottle will not satisfy the growing demands of a boy vigorously working and mischievously knocking about all the day round. To him more solid bread and butter are the diet. We need not be great intellectuals to understand that buttered toast, at the same time, would choke and kill an infant child.

Similarly here, work without self is healthy for the beginner, but a developed seeker needs more and more quietude and self-withdrawal for growing in his steady contemplation of the life within. Earlier, 'work without self' is the means; afterwards, 'work on Self' is the means. And the process is continued until, working or not working, through meditation it is realised that the Self alone is the essence in the ego which, till then, was recognised as the only reality.

In this sense of the term we can clearly know how ritualism has a definite place in the scheme of things as mapped out by the Vedantic seers of unimpeachable intellectual eminence.

'When is a man said to be Yogarudha—to have attained to Yoga?' The answer follows :

यदा हि नेन्द्रियार्थेषु न कर्मस्वनुषज्जते ।
सर्वसंकल्पसंन्यासी योगारूढस्तदोच्यते ॥ ४ ॥

4. *yadā hi ne'ndriyārtheṣu*
na karmsy ānuṣajjate
sarva-samkalpa-sannyāsī
yogārūḍhas tadocyate

यदा when, हि - verily, इन्द्रियार्थेषु – in sense–objects, न - not, कर्मसु – in actions, अनुषज्जते - *is attached,* सर्वसंकल्पसंन्यासी -renouncer of all thoughts, योगारूढ one who has attained to Yoga, तदा - *then,* उच्यते- is said.

4. When a man is not attached to sense-objects or to actions, having renounced all thoughts, then he is said to have attained to *Yoga.*

It is the experience of everyone and, therefore, it is not very difficult for a young seeker to know the state of an aspirant (*aruruksha*). It has been said by the Lord that, so long as we are in the state of seeking, the path of self-perfection lies through the highroad of selfless activity. Withdrawal from activity is to be undertaken only when you have reached the state of mental mastery (*Yogarudha*). To renounce activity at an earlier stage would be as unhealthy as to continue disturbing the mind with activities after having reached the second stage, where, we are told, quiescence is the means for gathering speed in our flight through meditation. Naturally, it is necessary for the seeker to know as to when exactly does he reach the second stage indicated here by the term *Yogarudha*.

In this stanza, Krishna is trying to indicate the physical and mental conditions of one who has come to brake the steed of mind and ride over it. He says that when one is feeling no mental attachment either to the sense-objects or to the actions in the outer world, it is one of the symptoms of one's own perfect mastery over the mind. This should not be over-stressed to a dreary literal meaning, making it a grotesque caricature of truth. It only means that the mind of a seeker in the meditation seat is so perfectly withdrawn from the external world of sense-objects and activities, that it is perfect in its equipoise at the time of its self-application. The sense-organs can run into the channels of the sense-objects only when the mind is flowing out to these organs. If the mind is kept engaged in the contemplation of a greater truth, providing for itself there, in the inner bosom, a larger quota of an ample joy, it will no more go hunting for bits of joys in the gutters of sensuality. A well-fed pet dog will not scrounge the public dustbins for its feed.

When the mind is not thus gushing out either through the sense-channels or through the fields of its egocentric activities, it becomes completely engaged in the contemplation of the greater truth-the Self. Here the term used to indicate complete non-attachment is to be noted very carefully. The Sanskrit word *anu-shajjate* is a word-symbol created by the prefix *anu* indicates 'not a bit'. Therefore, the term used here forbids even traces of attachment either to the sense-objects or to the fields of activity.

When a mind has been withdrawn from the sense-organs and completely detached from all its external physical activities, it is possible that it is still tossed and agitated by the gurglings of its own inner instincts of willing and wishing, desiring and earning. This power of *sankalpa* can bring more storms into the bosom of man than the disturbances his mind could receive from the external world. Krishna indicates here that he who has gained a complete mastery over his mind is one who has not only withdrawn himself from all sense-contacts and activities in the outer world, but has also dried up all the *sankalpa* disturbances,* in his own mind. Such an individual is, at the moment of meditation, in that inward-state which is described here as *Yogarudha*. It is clear that, to such an individual, meditation can be intensified only by quietude (*sama.*).

'When a man has attained Yoga, then the self is raised by the Self from out of the numerous evils of finite existence'. Therefore:

उद्धरेदात्मनाऽऽत्मानं नात्मानमवसादयेत् ।
आत्मैव ह्यात्मनो बन्धुरात्मैव रिपुरात्मनः ॥ ५ ॥

5. *uddhared ātmanā'tmānam*
nā'tmānam avasādayet
ātmaiva hy ātmano bandhur
ātmaiva ripur ātmanaḥ

उद्धरेत् -let (him) lift, आत्मना - by the self, आत्मानम् - the self, न-Not, आत्मानम् - the self, अवसादयेत्-let (him) lower, आत्मा-the Self, एव-only, हि-verily, आत्मनः - of the Self बन्धुः- friend, आत्मा - the Self, एव - only, रिपुः- the enemy, आत्मनः - of the Self.

5. Let a man lift himself by his own Self alone, and let him not lower himself; for, this Self alone is the friend of oneself, and this Self alone is the enemy of oneself.

As a complete *Sastra,* the Geeta has to be faithful to Truth and Truth alone, irrespective of what the tradition of the country had, at a given period, made the faithful ones believe. It is not very unhealthy to

---

* O Desire, I know where your roots lie. you are born of *sankalpa.* I shall not think of you, and you will cease to exist along with your roots.' — The *Mahabharata,* 'Santi Parva : 177–25.

believe that the grace from an external source is constantly helping a true seeker on his path of striving; but it is healthy only when this thought is correspondingly complemented with sufficiently intense individual self-effort. To believe that *guru*-grace will land on us by post in packets is against the *Sastras,* and the bigger the assertion with which such packets are presented, the more should we suspect the genuineness of the sender-saint.

Had there been a packet-method, we should have a 'packet-*Yoga*' explained in our scriptures; for our Rishis were exhaustive in their treatment of the science of self-perfection. If at all some great saints of today are sending *prasadams,* it is not to be considered and misconstrued that those packets are '*Atmic-powder*' which can be rubbed in through the skin between the eyebrows! With the right mental attitude, if we approach them and make use of them, certainly we can gain a certain amount of mental equipoise and self-confidence which can be intelligently applied in our own self-effort.

'Man should uplift himself by himself,' is the open statement declared by no less a person than Lord Krishna Himself-not cooed in a playful mood in the company of the Gopis of the Jamuna bank: at an hilarious hour of laughter and play, but roared to Arjuna on the battlefield at a serious moment of His life's fulfilment as an *avatar.* Man, if he wants to exalt himself into his greater cultural and spiritual possibilities now lying dormant in him, has to raise the lower in himself to the greater perfection that is the true and eternal central core in himself.

Everyone has in himself a picture of the ideal. This intellectual conception of ourselves is always very vivid in each one of us. But, unfortunately, this ideal remains only in the realm of thought, and not in the world of activity. Intellectually, we may have a clear and vivid picture of what we should be, but, mentally and physically, we behave as though we are the opposite of our own ideal concepts. The divorce between the 'idealistic-me' and the 'actual-me' is the measure of man's fall from his perfection.

Eighty per cent of us are generally unconscious of this dualism in ourselves. We mistake ourselves to be the *ideal,* and are generally blind to our own *actual* imperfections. Thus we find that a notoriously selfish man in society warmly and sincerely criticising the slightest traces of selfishness in his neighbour! In a world of no mirrors, it is possible that a squint-eyed man may come to laugh at another squint-eyed person, because the one who laughs knows not the angle in which his own eyeballs are facing each other!

Within ourselves, if we clearly watch, we can discover that intellectually we have a clear concept of morally strong, ethically perfect, physically loving, and socially disciplined ideal picture of the man that 'we should be', but in the mental zones of our emotions and feelings we are tantalised by our own attachments, likes and dislikes, loves and hatred, appetites and passions, and we behave like a cur fed by the wayside gutters, and ever quarrelling with others of the same ilk over dry and empty bones!

So long as the individual has not realised the existence of this dual personality in himself, there cannot be any religion for him. If an individual has discovered that there is 'enough in him to be divided into two portions,' and when he wants to keep the lower as brilliant and chaste as the higher, the technique that he will have to employ to fulfil this aspiration is called religion.

Mind is the saboteur that enchants us away from our own known perfection to be slave to the flesh and to the external objects of brittle satisfaction. Mind is the conditioning that distorts the ideal and creates the lower satanic sensuousself inus which is to be brought in unison with the intellect which is the equipment for the higher self to manifest. In short, when the rational and discriminative capacities of a limited intellect are brought to bear their authority upon the wavering and wandering sense-mongering mind, the lower is brought under discipline and made to attune itself with the noble and the divine in us. The processes by which the lower is brought under the direct management and discipline of the higher, are all together called the spiritual techniques.

This process of self-rehibilitation and self-redemption of the Satan in us cannot be executed through tenders and giving the contract to the lowest bidder. Each will have to do it all by himself unto himself; 'alone to the Alone all alone' is the way. No *guru* can take the responsibility; no scripture can promise this redemption, no alter can, with its divine blessings, make the lower the higher. The lower must necessarily be trained slowly and steadily to accept and come under the influence of the discipline of the higher. In this process, the teacher, the scripture, and the Houses-of-God all have their proper, appointed duties and limited influences. But the actual happening depends upon how far we ourselves learn to haul ourselves from the gutters of misunderstanding in us.

So far Bhagavan has indicated an exhaustive treatment which may be, in many of its aspects, considered equipment to the modern psychological process called introspection. Realising our own weaknesses, rejecting the false, asserting the better, and trying to live generally as best as we can the higher way of life is the process of introspection. But this is only a half of the entire process, and not the full swing.

The other half also is insisted upon here by Krishna. It is not only sufficient that we look within, come to note our weaknesses, erase them out, substitute the opposite good quality, and develop in our selves the better, but whatever little conquests we have made out of Satan's province, we must see to it that those areas are not again handed back to Satan's dominion. Warns Krishna almost in the same breath: *'Do not allow the self thereafter to fall down and be dragged again'* to the old level of the cheaper way of existence.

The second line of the stanza contains a glorious idea shaped into a beauty of expression which almost immortalises the great author Vyasa. We are to be considered both as our own friend and our own enemy. Any intelligent man observing and analysing life, will vouchsafe for the truth of the statement, but here more is meant philosophically than what greets the ear. Generally, we do not fully understand the import when we say that '*the Self is the friend of the self.*'

The lower in us can ever raise itself to the attunement of the higher, but the Higher can influence only when the lower is available for Its influence. To the extent the lesser in us surrenders itself to the influence of the Higher, to that extent It can serve the lower as a great friend. But if the lower refuses to come under the influence of the divine in us, the Divine Presence in us is accused of being an enemy of ourselves, inasmuch as the dynamism of life provides us its energy both for our 'life of higher aspirations' and for our 'life of low temptations.'

Ultimately, it is for the aspirant himself to accept the responsibility for blessing or damning himself. The potentiality for improvement, the chances for self-growth, the strength to haul ourselves from our own misconceptions about us—are all ever open for employment. But it all **depends** upon how we make use of them.

It has been said that 'he alone is the friend of himself, he alone is the enemy of himself'. Now it may be asked: 'What sort of a man is the friend of himself and what sort of a man is the enemy of himself? The answer follows :

बन्धुरात्माऽऽत्मनस्तस्य येनात्मैवात्मना जित: ।
अनात्मनस्तु शत्रुत्वे वर्तेतात्मैव शत्रुत्वे ॥ ६ ॥

6. *bandhur ātmā'tmanas tasya*
yenātmaivātmanā jitaḥ
anātmanas tu śatrutve
vartetātmaiva śatruvat

बन्धुः-friend, आत्मा-the self, आत्मन -of the self, तस्य-his, येन -by whom, आत्मा-the Self, एव - even, आत्मना - by the Self, जितः- is conquered, अनात्मनः - of unconquered self, तु - but, शत्रुत्वे - in the place of an enemy, वर्तेत- would remain, आत्मा-the Self, एव-even, शत्रुत्वम् -like an enemy.

6. The Self is the friend of the self for him who has conquered himself by the Self; but to the unconquered self, this Self stands in the position of an enemy like the (external) foe.

The Divine in us becomes our friend when, under its influence, the Satanic in us gets converted. To the extent the lower ego withdraws its identifications with the body and the sense-organs, feelings and ideas relating to the extrovert life, to that extent that given ego has come under the salutary influence of the nobler and the Divine. To such an ego, available for correction and proselytisation, the Self is a friend. But where the little-self remains a constant rebel against the higher, to that conquered self, the Divine Self is as if inimical in Its attitude towards the lower.

In short, the higher Self becomes a friend to the lower which is available for and which allows itself to be conquered by the higher influences and the Divine becomes inimical to the undivine when the lower limited-ego remains unconquered by the higher aspirations in us. This stanza is an elucidating annotation on the previous one.

Earlier, the state of the mental equipoise, called the Yogarudha, was explained. What exactly is the fulfilment of such a state in Yoga is being explained now.*

जितात्मन: प्रशान्तस्य परमात्मा समाहित: ।
शीतोष्णसुखदु: खेषु तथा मानापमानयो: ॥ ७ ॥

* Stanzas 3 and 4.

7. *jitātmanaḥ praśāntasya*
paramātmā samāhitaḥ
śītoṣṇa- sukha -duḥkheṣu
tathā mānāpamānayoḥ

जितात्मनः -of the self-controlled. प्रशान्तस्य-of the peaceful. परमात्मा- the Supreme Self, समाहितः-balanced, शीतोष्णसुखदु : खेषु - in cold and heat, pleasure and pain, तथा - as also, मानापमानयोः- in honour and dishonour.

7. The Supreme Self of him who is self-controlled and peaceful is balanced in cold and heat, pleasure and pain, as also in honour and dishonour.

When a seeker has come in his inner life to the state explained as *Yogarudha,* and when in that state of equipoise the mind is held steadfast in contemplation of the Supreme, the self-controlled one, in all serenity, is capable of maintining his consistency of meditation in all circumstances, favourable and adverse, at all levels of his personality. In the second line of the stanza, it is clearly indicated that no excuse in the world is sufficiently strong to justify a seeker's inability to continue keeping the awareness of his Eternal Nature in himself.

Three pairs-of- opposites are indicated here as (1) heat and cold; (2) joy and sorrow; (3) honour and dishonour. In the enumeration of these three teams of conditions, Krishna is exhausting, through the mention of the types, all the possible threats that an individual may receive from the outer world against his equipoise and tranquillity.

'Heat and Cold': These are stimuli that are felt and experienced by the body at the body level. Whether in heat or in cold, thoughts, we know, do not expand or shrink, and the ideas cannot shiver or perspire. All these reactions can be only in the body and, therefore, Krishna is indicating by this pair all the vicissitudes that may visit the body, such as, health and disease, youth and old age, etc.

By the second pair-of-opposites indicated here, ***'pleasure and pain',*** the Lord is symbolically indicating all the destinies suffered at the mental zone. Pleasure and pain are experienced not by the body, but always by the mind. It includes all the tyrannies of our different emotions which might threaten the mental arena at one time or the other in a man's life. Hatred and love, affection and jealousy, kindness and cruelty... a thousand varieties of emotions may storm the 'within'; but none of them is an excuse, according to Krishna, for the diligent and the sincere to lose hold of himself from steadfastness in his contemplation.

Similarly also, the last pair-of-opposites, indicated as '*honour and dishonour',* shows how no threat of any storm in the intellectual zone is a sufficient plea to condone or sympathise with an individual who has fallen away from the state of Perfection. Honour and dishonour are evaluated upon and reacted with only by the intellect.

Thus, by these three representative pairs-of-opposites from the three worlds of the body, the mind, and the intellect, Krishna is trying to exhaust all possibilities of obstacles in man's life, and then he adds that in all such conditions the Supreme Self is to be the object of constant realisation for one who is perfectly self-controlled and serene. He ever remains unruffled in all circumstances—favourable or unfavourable; in all environments—good or bad; in all companies—wise or foolish.

'What is the glory of such an individual? What does he become by such a process? Why should he go through such a gruelling inward training and self-discipline?

ज्ञानविज्ञानतृप्तात्मा कूटस्थो विजितेन्द्रियः ।
युक्त इत्युच्यते योगी समलोष्टाश्मकाञ्चनः ॥ ८ ॥

8. *jñāna-vijñāna-tṛptātmā*
kūṭastho vijitendriyaḥ
yukta ity ucyate yogī
sama-loṣṭāśma-kāñcanaḥ

ज्ञानविज्ञानतृप्तात्मा - one who is satisfied with knowledge and wisdom (Self-realisation), कूटस्थः - unshaken, विजितेन्द्रियः - who has conquered the senses, युक्तः - united or harmonised, इति - thus, उच्यते - is said, योगी - Yogi, समलोष्टाश्मकाञ्चनः - one to whom a lump of earth, a stone, and gold are the same.

8. The *Yogi* who is satisfied with knowledge and wisdom, who remains unshaken, who has conquered the senses, to whom a lump of earth, a stone, and gold are the same, is said to be harmonised, i.e., he is said to have attained *nirvikalpa samadhi.*

Such an individual, self-controlled and serene, who has come to contemplate constantly upon the nature of the Self as understood from the *Sastras,* through all his circumstances in life, soon becomes, says

Krishna, filled with a divine satisfaction and becomes an unshakable *Yogin.* Here the satisfaction is not merely the joy that a true and intelligent man comes to enjoy when he carefully studies and masters Vedanta, but, according to Krishna, a true *Yogin* comes to experience a satisfied contentment which is much superior to the thrilled joys experienced in all intense studies.

The knowledge gained through study is indicated here by the term *gyana,* and the first-hand experience gained by the seeker of the Self in himself is called the knowledge of direct perception, which is termed here, in the Geeta vocabulary, as *vigyana.**

Kootastha (Unchanging, Immutable): This is the term used for the Eternal Self. Its exrpressiveness becomes apparent when we understand that the term '*koota*' means in Sanskrit the 'anvil'. The anvil is that upon which the blacksmith places his red-hot iron-bits and hammers them into the required shapes. In spite of the hammerings, nothing happens to the anvil, as the anvil resists all modification and change but allows all other things to get changed while in contact with it. Thus, the term '*kootastha*' means that which 'remains anvil-like', and though itself suffers no change, it makes others change.

He is a saint and has the full-blown fragrance who has sought and discovered a perfect contentment which arises out of his subjective experience of what the ***Sastra*** says and has come in contact with the Self that changes not. And such a saint becomes tranquil and a master of equal-vision in all conditions of his life. To him, a clod of mud, a precious stone, and costly gold are all the same. This equanimity of mind in profit and loss, at the acquisition of precious things, or at the presentation of mere filth, is the very test to show that the individual has spiritually evolved and that, to him, no gain can bring any extra joy, nor loss any extra sorrow!

In my dream I earned a lot of wealth, but ere I enjoyed it fully, I woke up to my waking state, poverty. In my destitution, when I am suffering the pangs of hunger, I will not feel, in any sense of the term, consoled by the thought that I was rich in my dream and that in my dream-bank, in its dream-vaults, I had my dream-riches! Similarly, to a master who has gained perfection, transcended the world of the mind-and-intellect, and achieved the true awakening of the soul, thereafter a lump of earth, a

* This is Sankara's interpreation, and the Acharya distinguishes *gyana* from *vigyana* inasmuch as, according to this father of modern Vedanta, *gyana* is 'book knowledge' and *vigyana* is 'wisdom gained through direct realization of the things so taught'.

piece of gold, or a precious stone of this world are all equally futile things. They cannot add even a jot of extra joy or pain unto him. He has become the sole proprietor of the Bliss Absolute. To Kubera, the treasurer of the heavens,even a kingdom on the globe is no profit which can make him dance in ecstasy!

सुहृन्मित्रार्युदासीनमध्यस्थद्वेष्यबन्धुषु ।
साधुष्वपि च पापेषु समबुद्धिर्विशिष्यते ॥ ९ ॥

'Moreover....'

9. suhṛn-mitrāry-udāsīna
madhyastha-dveṣya-bandhuṣu
sādhuṣv api ca pāpeṣu
sama-buddhir viśiṣyate

सुहृन्मित्रार्युदासीनमध्यस्थद्वेष्यबन्धुषु- in the good -hearted, in friends, in enemies, in the indifferent, in neutrals, in haters, and in relatives, साधुषु in the reghteous, अपि-also, च-and, पापेषु -in the unrighteous, समबुद्धिः-one who has equal mind, विशिष्यते -excels.

9. He who is of the same mind to the good-hearted friends, enemies, the indifferent, the neutral, the hateful, relatives, the righteous and the unrighteous, excels.

In the previous stanza it was indicated that the Man of Perfection develops equal-vision as far as the things of the world are concerned. The universe is not made of things alone, but is consituted of beings also. Now the doubt arises: what will be the relationship between a perfect man of equipoise with the living kingdom of beings around him? Will he negate the whole lot as unreal? In his preoccupations with experience of the Eternal and the Immortal, which is the substratum for the entire world of changing phenomenal beings, will he ignore to serve the world and help the living generation? The idea is taken up here for discussion.

Such a man of excellence, Krishna says, regards all relationship with an equal love and consideration, be they '*friends, or foes, or the indifferent, or the neutral, or the hateful, or the nearest Relations.* 'In his equal-vision all of them are equally important, and he embrances with his infinite heart all of them in the same warmth and ardour. His love knows no distinction between the righteous and the bad. To him a sinner is but an ego living in its misunderstandings, since sin is only a mistake of the soul and not a positive blasphemy against Itself. Rama Tirtha beautifully expresses it when he says that 'we are punished *by* the sin and not *for* it.'

In the right understanding of his own Self and the resulting realisation of his own Self. he becomes the Self everywhere, and he discovers a unity in the perceived diversity and a subtle rhythm in the obvious discord in the world outside. To him who has realised himself to be the Self which is all-pervading, the entire universe becomes his own Self and, therefore, his relationship with every other part of the universe is equal and same. Whether I get wounded in the hand or the leg, on the back or in the front, on the head or the shoulder, it is the same to me since I am identifying myself equally with my head, my trunk, and my legs.

'Through what methods can one attain this highest goal and assure for oneself the surest result?' It is explained:

योगी युञ्जीत सततमात्मानं रहसि स्थित: ।
एकाकी यतचित्तात्मा निराशीरपरिग्रह: ॥१०॥

10. *yogī yuñjīta satatam*
ātmānam rahasi sthitaḥ
ekākī yata cittātmā
nirāśīr aparigrahaḥ

योगी - the Yogi, युञ्जीत - let him keep the mind steady, सततम् - Constantly, आत्मानम् - self रहसि - in solitude, स्थित: - remaining, एकाकी - alone, यतचित्तात्मा - one with the mind and body controlled, निराशी - free from hope, अपरिग्रह: - free from greed.

10. Let the Yogi try constantly to keep the mind steady, remaining in solitude, alone with the mind and body controlled, free from hope and greed.

The last few stanzas expound and explain such a wondrous goal of life that no reader of the Geeta with intelligence and enthusiasm can stand away from the compelling charm of its beauteous face. Arjuna seems to have expressed an eagerness to know the ways and means by which this indomitable inward equilibrium can be achieved by him for his own constant experience. As an answer to his eager looks, Krishna explains in his own words how an individual can slowly grow to maintain himself finally in this spirit of consummate love for all, at all times.

Krishna is conceived in the *Mahabharata* as a voluntary manifestation of the Supreme, and hence he is addressed as Sri Krishna *Paramatman.* He is giving here an advice to his most intimate friend and companion. Arjuna, on the methods of self-development and the techniques of self-perfection. Even then it is not said that the Lord would give him a secret method by which the seeker would not have to make any struggle at all, and that the entire·responsibility would be borne by the Creator of the universe. The very opening words of the stanza weed out any such false hopes in the minds of the seekers: *'O man of self-control (Yogi), you should constantly practise concentration.'* It is only through the practice of meditation that a mortal can grow out of his weaknesses and flower forth culturally into the greater perfection-possibilities within himself.

Details of how the meditation is to be conducted are given in the rest of the stanza : *'Sitting in solitude'* one should practise meditation. The word has been unnecessarily so overstretched in recent times in India that the term 'meditation' brings a sense of horror and fear into the minds of the new seekers. It does not mean that meditation can be practised only in the jungles and in solitary caves. It only means that in our homes the seeker should try to withdraw himself from his mental and physical preoccupations and retire to a corner in his house for the purpose of his early meditation.

Solitude can be gained only when there is a mental withdrawal from the world outside. One who is full of desires and constantly meditating upon the sense-objects cannot hope to gain any solitude even in a virgin forest. Again, the word solitude *(rahasi)* rings a meaning of secretiveness, indicating that religion should not be a boradcast of self-advertisement, but must be set of true values of life secretly practised within the heart, ordering our way of thinking and encouraging our pursuit of the nobler values of life. Physically alone *(ekaki)* for the purposes of meditation, when one strives, his success in his inward quietude will be directly proportional to the amount of self-control he is practising in his daily life. Self-control is not possible unless we know how to free ourselves from 'eagerness to possess' and 'anxiety to hoard'. To renounce our preoccupations with our endless plans for possessing more is indicated here by the term 'free from hope' *(nirasi)*. And the term 'free from possession' *(aparigraha)* indicates all our anxieties in saving, hoarding, and protecting what we possess.

When one, well-established in these necessary physical self-controls, unavoidable mental and intellectual habits, sits meditating upon the Truth in all secrecy, he is a true seeker striving on the right path to achieve and acquire the highest that is possible in life.

'Now, in the sequel, the Lord proceeds to prescribe for the Yoga-practitioner particular modes of sitting, eating, recreation and such other aids to Yoga.' First of all, he explains the mode of sitting as follows :

शुचौ देशे प्रतिष्ठाप्य स्थिरमासनमात्मनः ।
नात्युच्छ्रितं नातिनीचं चैलाजिनकुशोत्तरम् ॥ ११ ॥

11. *śucau deśe pratiṣṭhāpya*
sthiram āsanam ātmanaḥ
nātyucchitam nā'tinīc am
cailājina -kuśottaram

शुचौ - in a clean, देशे - spot, प्रतिष्ठाप्य - having established, स्थिरम् - firm, आसनम् - seat, आत्मनः - his own, न - not, अत्युच्छ्रितम् - very high, न - not, अतिनीचम् - very low, चैलजिनकुशोत्तरम् - a cloth, skin, and Kusa-grass one over the other.

11. Having in a clean spot established a firm seat of his own, neither too high nor too low, made of a cloth, a skin, and *Kusa*-grass, one over the other.

If meditation is the path by which one can gain tranquillity and equal-vision within oneself, it is necessary that, in this text-book of self-perfection, Lord Krishna should give a complete and exhaustive explanation of the technique of meditation. In order to fulfil this demand, hereunder we get a few verses explaining the position, the means, and the end of a meditator at his work.

In these words is a description of the seat and the place for perfect meditation. '*In a clean place*': It is important inasmuch as the external conditions have a direct bearing upon the human mind. In a clean place there is more chance for the seekers to maintain a cleaner mental condition. Apart from this, commentators explain that the place should be rid of mosquitoes, house-flies, bugs, ants, and such other creatures that may disturb the beginner's mental concentration which he is trying to turn inward. Also, cleanliness is considered as next to Divinity in India—not, of course, in our modern times of total Hindu decadence, where a typical '*bhakta*' is a stinking specimen of dirt and ugliness!

In his seat the meditator is asked to sit steady (*sthiram*). Without moving the physical body at every short interval, and without swinging the body either forward and backward or sideways, the seeker is asked to get himself firmly established on his seat because physical movement contributes immensely to the shattering of the mental concentration and inner equipoise. This is very well realised by every one of us if we only remember our attitude when we are sincerely and seriously thinking over something. In order to get established in a firm posture, it would be advisable to sit in any 'comfortable seat (asana), with the vertebral column erect, fingers interlocked, and hands thrown in front.*

Adding more details, Krishna says that the seat of meditation 'should not be too high or too low'. If it is too high, there will be a sense of insecurity in the meditator, created as a result of his instinct of self-preservation, and he will find it difficult to extricate himself from his outer-world-consciousness and plunge himself into the inner. Again, we are told that the seat should not be too low: this is to avoid the mistake of meditating in any damp underground cellar, where chances are that the seeker may easily develop rheumatic pains in his body. During meditation the heart becomes slightly slow and, to the extent we are withdrawn into ourselves, even the blood pressure falls. At such a time of low resistance, if the place be damp, there is a great chance of a seeker developing pains in his joints. To avoid such troubles, the warning is given here.

When the Geeta is out to give details, she leaves nothing to the imagination of the student. The exhaustive details regarding the ideal seat to sit for meditation is an example. It is said here that a mattress of Kusa-grass on the ground, with a deerskin covered with a piece of cloth on top of it, is the perfect seat for long meditations. Dampness is avoided by the Kusa-grss which keeps the seat warm during winter. In summer the skin becomes too hot, as some seekers are allergic to the animal skin, especially when their skin has become slightly moist with perspiration. This contingency is being avoided by spreading over the skin a piece of clean cloth. Having thus established himself firmly on the meditation-seat prepared as above, what exactly he is to do mentally and intellectually is now to be explained.

'What should be done after establishing oneself on the prepared seat?'

तत्रैकाग्रं मनः कृत्वा यतचित्तेन्द्रियक्रिय: ।
उपविश्यासने युञ्ज्याद्योगमात्मविशुद्धये ॥ १२ ॥

> 12. tatraikāgram manaḥ krtvā
> yata -cittendriya -kriyaḥ
> upaviśyāsane yuñjyād
> yogam ātma -viśuddhaye

---

* See Swamiji's *Meditation and Life.*

तत्र - there, एकाग्रम् - one-pointed, मनः - the mind, कृत्वा - having made, यतचित्तेन्द्रियक्रियः - one who has controlled the actions of the mind and the senses, उपविश्य, - being seated, आसने - on the seat, युञ्ज्यात् - let him practise, योगम् - Yoga, आत्मविशुद्धये - for the purification of the self.

12. There, having made the mind one-pointed, with the actions of the mind and the senses controlled, being seated on the seat, let him practise *Yoga* for the purification of the self.

However scientifically prepared it may be, to sit on an appropriate *asana (*seat) is not in itself *Yoga.* The appropriate physical condition is conducive to generating the right mental attitude for the spiritual practices, but a mere physical posture cannot in itself guarantee any spiritual self-development.

In this verse, Krishna is giving what the seeker should practise in his seat of meditation. Having brought the body steadfast in posture and steady, how one should employ his mind and intellect in the **process** of divine contemplation and meditation, is the theme which is being discussed here. The first instruction given is that *'you should make the mind single-pointed'*. This instruction cannot be worked out by a seeker unless he knows how he can bring about this necessary inward condition in himself. It is very cheap and easy for a *rishi* to advise the members of the confused generation to make their mind integrated.

Such an advice, when not sufficiently supported by practical details, becomes a mere high-sounding philosophy, and not a useful guidance for the seekers. The Geeta being a textbook which translates philosophy into life, in its typical spirit here the stanza immediately explains how we can bring the mind to an ideal single-pointedness.

'*Subduing the faculty of imagination and the activities of the sense-organs'*— is the instruction given by Krishna. Single-pointedness is the very potent nature of the mind, but it gets flabbergasted, confused, and even mad when it gets dynamised by either the inner force of one's own surging imagination or the outward pull rendered by the hallucinations of the sense-organs. If these two avenues of dissipation are blocked, instantaneously the mind becomes, of its own nature, single-pointed.

Thus, seated on the earlier prepared meditation-seat, and making the mind single-pointed through the process of subduing mental imaginations and controlling the wildness of the sense-organs, the seeker is encouraged to practise *Yoga.* To keep the single-pointed mind constantly on the steady contemplation of the Ultimate Self is the inner *Yoga* that has been mentioned here.

Naturally, every seeker would have rightly a desire to know why he should meditate thus. In order to remove all misunderstandings from the heart of meditators that they would be thereby directly coming face to face with the *Atman,* Krishna here appends to the verse the effects of such meditation. Through steady and regular meditation, the *Sastra* promises only inner purification. Agitations in the mind are its impurities. A purified mind is that which has no agitations, and when the mind has thus become pure and steady, the Consciousness, looking at the steady reflection of itself, comes to rediscover Its own real nature. This process is similar to the technique by which we understand ourselves while consulting our own reflection made in a mirror.

'The external seat has been described. Now, what should be the posture of the body? Listen....'

समं कायशिरोग्रीवं धारयन्नचलं स्थिरः ।
संप्रेक्ष्य नासिकाग्रं स्वं दिशश्चानवलोकयन् ॥ १३ ॥

13. samam kāya-śiro-grīvam
dhārayann acalam sthiraḥ
samprekṣya nāsikāgram svam
diśaś cānavalokayan

समम् - erect, कायशिरोग्रीवम् - body, head, and neck, धारयन् - holding · अचलम् - still, स्थिर: - steady, संप्रेक्ष्य - gazing at, नासिकाग्रम् - tip of the nose, स्वम् - one's own, दिश: - directions, च - and, अनवलोकयन् - not looking.

13. Let him firmly hold his body, head, and neck erect and still, gazing at the tip of his nose, without looking around.

After describing in all detail the arrangement of the seat of meditation and how to sit there properly, Lord Krishna had already explained what the meditator should do with his mind and intellect. He said earlier that the mind should be made single-pointed by subduing all the activities of the sense-organs and the imagination. Adding more detail to the technique of meditation, it is now said that the meditator should firmly hold his body in such a fashion that his vertebral column is completely erect. The head and the neck should be erect, and in this posture, which is geometrically perpendicular to the horizontal seat upon which the Yogi is firmly settling himself, it is pointedly indicated that he should hold his body 'firmly'.

This term should not be misunderstood as holding the body in all tension. 'Firmly' here means not that the body should be held stiffly, but that the relaxed body must be held in such a fashion that there should not be in the physical structure any tendecny to swing forward and backward, or sideways from right to left.

The seeker, having thus fixed himself ready for the meditation should, it is added here, *'gaze at the tip of his nose'*. This does not mean that an individual should with half-opened eyes, deliberately turn his eyeballs towards the 'tip of his own nose'. There are many seekers who had come to suffer much physical discomforts, such as, headaches, giddiness, exhaustion, tension, etc., because they had tried to follow this instruction verbatim. Sankara, in his commentary, has definitely given us the right direction. He says that the term here means only that the meditator, while meditating, should have his attention *'as though turned towards the tip of his own nose'*. That this interpretation is not a laboured and artificial intellectualism of the Acharya is clearly borne out by the following phrase in the second line.

'Not looking around': This instruction clearly shows what was in the mind of Krishna when he gave the insturction that the meditator should take his post on this sacred seat and direct his entire attention towards the tip of his own nose—so that he may not get himself dissipated in his attention and wander all round. Where the eyes go, there the mind faithfully follows: this is the law. That is why when an individual is rather confused we find that his gaze is not steady. Many a time we judge another individual as behaving funny or suspicious, and in all such cases our evidence is nothing other than the unsteadiness in the gaze of the individual concerned. Watch anyone who is indecisive and who is unsteady in his determination, and you can immediately observe that the individual's looks are definitely unsteady and confusedly wandering.

'Moreover....'

प्रशान्तात्मा विगतभीर्ब्रह्मचारिव्रते स्थित: ।
मन: संयम्य मच्चित्तो युक्त आसीत मत्पर: ॥ १४ ॥

14. praśāntātmā vigatabhīr
brahmacāri-vrate sthitaḥ
manaḥ samyamya maccitto
yukta āsita matparaḥ

प्रशान्तात्मा - serene minded, विगतभीः - fearless ब्रह्मचरिव्रते - in the vow of Brahmacharya, स्थितः - firm, मनः - the mind, संयम्य - having controlled, मच्चित्तः - thinking of Me, युक्तः - balanced, आसीत - let him sit, मत्परः - as the supreme goal.

14. Serene-minded, fearless, firm in the vow of Brahmacharya, having controlled the mind, thinking of Me and balanced, let him sit, having Me as the Supreme Goal.

When the meditator has thus practised meditation for a certain period of time, as a result of his practice, in his mind he comes to experience a larger share of quietude and peace. This extremely subtle form of inward peace is indicated here by the term *'prasanta'*. This inward silence, revelling in an atmosphere of extreme joy and contentment, is the exact situation in which the individual can be trained to express the nobler and the divine qualities which are inherent in the Divine Self.

A meditator invariably finds it difficult to scale the higher realms of experience due to a sheer psychological fear complex. As the *Yogin* slowly and steadily gets himself unwound from his sensuous *vasanas,* he gets himself released, as it were, from the cruel embrace of his own mental octopus. At this moment of transcendence the unprepared seeker feels himself morally afraid of the thought that he is getting himself dissolved away into '*nothingness*'. The ego, in its long habits of living in close proximity with its own limitations, finds it hard even to believe that there is an existence Supreme, Divine and Infinite. One is reminded of the story of the stranded fisher-women who complained that they could not get any sleep at all when they had to spend the night in a perfumery shop till they put their baskets very near their nose ! Away from our pains, we dread to enter the Infinite Bliss !

This sense of fear is the death-knell of all spiritual progress. Even if progress were to reach the bosom of such an individual, he will be compelled to reject it because of the rising storm of subjective fear in himself. Even though the mind has become extremely peaceful and joyous, and has renounced all its sense of fear through the study of the scriptures and continuous practise of regular meditation, the progress is not assured, and even a guarantee of failure shall ever be hanging over the head of the seeker, unless he struggles hard to get himself established in perfect *brahmacharya.*

'The asceticism of Brahmacharya': Here the word implies not only its Upanishadic implications, but definitely something more original, especially when it comes from Lord Krishna's mouth, and that too in the context of the Geeta. *Brahmacharya,* generally translated as 'the vow of celibacy', has a particular meaning, but the term has also a wider and more general implication. *Brahmacharya* is not only the control of the sex-impulses but is also the practice of self-control in all avenues of sense-impulses and sense-satisfactions. Unless the seeker has built up a perfect cage of intelligent self-control, the entire world-of-objects shall flood into the bosom, to bring therein a supreme state of unending chaos. A mind agitated thus by the inflow of the sense-objects is a mind that is completely dissipated and ruined.

Apart from this meaning, which is essentially indicative of the goal, or rather, a state of complete detachment from the mind's courtings with the external world-of-objects, there is a deeper implication to this significant and famous term. *Brahmacharya* as such is a term that can be dissolved to mean 'wandering in *Brahmavichar.'* To engage our mind in the contemplation of the Self, the Supreme Reality, is the saving factor that can really help us in withdrawing our mind from the external objects.

The human mind must have one field or the other to engage itself. Unless it is given some inner field to meditate upon, it will not be in a position to retrieve itself from its extrovert preoccupations. This is the secret behind all success in 'total celibacy'. The successful Indian *Yogi* need not be gazed at as a rare phenomenon in nature, and his success can be the success of all people if only they know how to get themselves established in this inward self-control. It is because people are ignorant of the positive methods to be practised for a continuous and successful negation and complete rejection of the charm of the sense-organs, that they invariably fail in their endeavour.

Here, the secret method of living in *brahmacharya* is indicated by the very same term as an instruction. In fact, *brahmacharya* is a 'bisexual term', capable of self-fertilisation ! In the very same term we have a happy marriage of both instruction and prescription. Generally, in the scriptural texts we have portions wherein the teachers' instructions of what ought to be done are invariably followed by a complete and detailed prescription of how the 'instruction portion' (*vidhi*) can be faithfully availed of and followed. But, in the case of the term *brahmacharya,* we have in it at once the 'instruction' on what ought to be done and also the 'prescription' as to how best it can be done.

Naturally, it becomes easy for the individual who has gained in himself all the three above-mentioned qualities to control and direct the newfound energies in himself. The inward peace, an attribute of the intellect, comes only when the discriminative faculty is relatively quiet. Fearlessness brings about a large control over the exhaustive thought-commotions in the mental zone. *Brahmacharya,* in its aspect of sense-withdrawal, lends a larger share of physical quietude. Therefore, when by the above process the intellect, mind, and body are all controlled and brought to the maximum amount of peace and quietude, the 'way of life' pursued by the seeker provides for him a large saving in the mental energy which would have been otherwise spent away in sheer dissipation.

This newly discovered and fully availed strength makes the mind stronger and stronger, so that the seeker experiences in himself a growing capacity to withdraw his wandering mind into himself and to fix his entire thoughts 'in the contemplation of Me, the Self'.

The concluding instruction in this most significant verse in the chapter is: *Let him sit in Yoga, having Me as his Supreme Goal.* It has been already said in the earlier chapter that the meditator should continue meditation, and erelong (*achirat*) he will have the fulfilment of his meditation. The same idea is suggested here. Having made the mind tame, and keeping it away from its own endless dissipations, we are instructed to keep the single-pointed mind in the contemplation of the Divine and His Eternal Nature in the Self. Immediately following this instruction is the order that he should remain in this attitude of meditation seeking nothing else but *'Me as the Supreme Goal'* Erelong, in the silence and quietude within, the withering mind and other equipments shall exhaust themselves, and the seeker shall wake up to realise his own Infinite, Eternal, Blissful, and quiet nature, the Self.

युञ्जन्नेवं सदाऽऽत्मानं योगी नियतमानस: ।
शान्तिं निर्वाणपरमां मत्संस्थामधिगच्छति ॥ १५ ॥

15. *yuñjonn evam sadā'tmānam*
yogi niyata-mānasaḥ
śāntim nirvāṇa-paramām
mat-samsthām adhigacchati

युञ्जन् - balancing, एवम् - thus, सदा - always, आत्मानम् - the self, योगी - yogi, नियतमानसः - one with the controlled mind, शान्तिम् - to peace, निर्वाण परमाम् - that which culminates in *nirvana* (*moksha*) , मत्संस्थम् - abiding in Me, अधिगच्छति - attains.

15. Thus, always keeping the mind balanced, the Yogi, with his mind controlled, attains to the Peace abiding in Me, which culminates in total liberation (*nirvana or moksha*).

After describing thus the physical pose, the mental stability, and the consequent intellectual self-application, the Lord,on the Kurukshetra, is describing the last lap in the technique of meditation to His beloved friend, the Pandava prince. When all the above details are worked out in anyone, that individual becomes a man steadfast both in his physical and subtler life, and, thereby, he comes to release from himself a large quantity of his psychic vitality. In this stanza it is told that when a meditator controls his mind and 'constantly' (*sada*) keeps his mind away from its agitations, it is such an individual who could easily and surely reach the Supreme.

The term 'always' (*sada*) should not be misunderstood as suggesting that the practitioner should thereby come to live criminally neglecting all his duties towards his home and his world around himself. Here the term 'always' only connotes 'a duration of constant and consistent inner silence' during one's meditation. At the peak of meditation, the practitioner comes to a point of perfect and still 'halt'.* The following stanza explains what happens in the still moment when the mind is perfectly calmed.

The individual comes to experience an infinite peace which is *'the peace that resides in him'*. The Self is Peace Absolute (*santam*) inasmuch as the processes of mental agitations, intellectual disturbances, and physical excitements are not there in It since It is beyond these matter envelopments. In this portion of the stanza it may look as though Krishna is advocating the dualistic school of philosophy, since here it is said that 'the meditator *reaches* the peace that is My own nature.' To conceive of a Truth having qualities is to reduce the Eternal to the finite status of a substance (*dravya*). Again if the meditator experiences *'the peace that resides in Me'*, then the goal gained becomes an 'object' different from the meditator.

---

* See Swamiji's *Meditation and Life.*

The subtle philosopher, Sri Krishna, rcognised this unavoidable imperfection of the spoken language and, therefore, tries to neutralize the fallacy in his expression by the significant term, 'the peace that ultimately culminates in the supreme liberation' (*nirvana-para-mam*).

In short, when the meditator has come to the moment of perfect silence within, he comes to experience, at first, a peace that is unknown in the world without, and soon, as it were the experiencer gets slowly acted upon and digested into the very substance of the Truth whose fragrance was the Peace which the dying ego of the meditator, in its gasping delusion, seemed to experience at the gateway to its own Real Divine Nature. In short, in the last stage of fulfilment in meditation, the meditator 'awakens' to his own status of Self-hood. The *Advaita* experience is the one sole factor that had been repeated at all hands all over Krishna's Song Divine.

'The following are the regulations as regards the meditator's food, etc.'

नात्यश्नतस्तु योगोऽस्ति न चैकान्तमनश्नतः ।
न चातिस्वप्नशीलस्य जाग्रतो नैव चार्जुन ॥ १६ ॥

16. nā'tyaśnatas tu yogo'sti
na caikāntam anaśnataḥ
na cāti svapna-sīlasya
jāgrato naiva cā'rjuna

न - not, अत्यश्नतः-of one who eats too much, तु - verily, योगः-Yoga, अस्ति -is, न -not, च -and, एकान्तम् - at all, अनश्नतः-of one who does not eat, न - not, च - and, अतिस्वप्नशीलस्य - of one who sleeps too much, जाग्रतः - one who is awake, न - not, एव - even, च - and, च - and, अर्जुन - O Arjuna.

16. Verily, Yoga is not possible for him who eats too much, nor for him who does not eat at all, nor for him who sleeps too much, nor for him who is (always) awake, O Arjuna.

When the above technique and goal are so clearly given out, one is apt to wonder at one's own incapacity to reach anywhere near the indicated goal in spite of the fact that one has been sincerely and constantly meditating for a number of years. What is exactly the behaviour in a seeker that unconsciously takes him away from the grand road to success? No scientific theory is complete unless it enumerates the various precautions that are to be taken for achieving complete success. The stanza under review and the following ones together give a warning of all the possible pitfalls on the path of *Dhyana Yoga*.

Moderation in indulgences and activities at all levels of one's personality is an unavoidable prerequisite which alone can assure true success in meditation. Intemperateness would bring discordant and riotous agitations in the various layers of matter, shattering the harmonious melody in the life of integration. Therefore, strict moderation in food, sleep, and recreation is enjoined: everything should be well measured and completely defined.

'Yoga is not possible for him who eats too much nor for him who does not eat at all.' —Here, the term 'eat' should be understood as including in its all-comprehensive meaning all sense-enjoyments, mental feelings, and intellectual perceptions. It is not only the process of consuming things through the mouth; it includes the enjoyments gained through all the avenues of sense-perceptions and inward experiences.

There is a lot of confusion regarding the advisability or otherwise of certain types of food. Seekers generally get too much confused with the problem of what to eat and what not to eat. Perhaps to remove this idea. Sankara, in his commentary, quotes a relevant advice given in the *Satapatha Brahmana:* 'Whatever food is suited to oneself that protects, it injures not. A greater quantity injures and a smaller quantity protects not. 'In fact, if the above quotation explains what to eat, ***Patanjali*** *Yogasastra* clearly gives right direction to all meditators on how much to eat.*

Drawing our conclusions from these standards, we may understand the rule to be: 'Eat whatever comes to us handy, without creating unnecessary destruction to the living kingdom just for our personal existence, and consume an intelligent quantity which does not load our stomach.' This is the golden rule of dieting for a successful meditator.

It is rightly said that neither 'too much of sleep' — which unnecessarily dullens our faculties and renders the individual more and more gross—nor 'no sleep at all' is the right policy for a student in the spiritual life. Intelligent moderation is the law.

This stanza might confuse the dull-witted and, therefore, the following verse answers the question: *How then can Yoga be achieved?'*

युक्ताहारविहारस्य युक्तचेष्टस्य कर्मसु ।
युक्तस्वप्नावबोधस्य योगो भवति दु:खहा ॥ १७ ॥

---

* Pantanjali insists that half (the stomach) should be for food and condiments, the third (quarter) for water, and the fourth should be reserved for the free movement of air.

17. yuktāhāra-vihārasya
yukta-ceṣtasya karmasu
yukta-svapnāvabodhasya
yogo bhavati duḥkhahā

युक्ताहारविहारस्य - of one who is moderate in eating and recreation, युक्तचेष्टस्य-कर्मसु - of one who is moderate in exertion in actions, युक्तस्वप्नावबोधस्य-of one who is moderate in sleep and wakefulness, योग: - Yoga, भवति - becomes, दु:खहा - the destroyer of pain.

17. Yoga becomes the destroyer of pain for him who is moderate in eating and recreation, who is moderate in his exertion during his actions, who is moderate in sleep and wakefulness.

This stanza plans the favourable life, living which *Yoga* can more successfully be cultivated. Moderation in eating and recreation, in sleep and activities, is the prescription that has been insisted upon by the Lord of *Yoga.*

In indicating the blessed life of temperance and self-control, Krishna has used such select vocabulary that the words have the fragrant note of an ampler suggestiveness. An ordinary seeker takes to some sacred work in a misguided belief that 'selfless work' could create in him more worthiness for his spiritual life. In this false notion, many seekers have I met, who have in the long run fallen a prey to their own activities. In this stanza we have a clear direction as to how to avoid the victimization of ourselves by the work that we undertake.

Not only is it sufficient, implies Krishna, that we must be temperate—discriminately careful in choosing the right field of activity —but we must also see that the *efforts* that we put into that activity are moderate (*cheshtasya).* Having selected a divine work, if in its programme of effort we get ourselves bound and enslaved, the chances are that the work, instead of redeeming us from our existing *vasanas,* would create in us more and more new tendencies and, in the exhaustion created by the work, we would sink slowly into agitations and, perhaps, even into animalism.

When Krishna wants to indicate the absolute necessity for moderation regarding sleep and wakefulness, the phrases which he uses are very significant. *'Svapna'* is the term used for indicating the total conscious life of the ego's active experiences in the world. Elsewhere in the Upanishads also* the entire life's experiences have been classified under the 'state of sleep' (the *non*apprehension of Reality) and the 'state of dream' (the *misa*apprehension of Reality) wherein the waking state is also found to be included. Reading the same meaning of the *Karika* into the term *svapna* used here by the Divine Charioteer, we can easily find that the wakefulness ***(avabodha)*** mentioned here is a happy complementary term to *svapna.* The terms altogether mean more than what greets the ear.

The term *avabodha* used here echoes the scriptural goal explained therein as Absolute Knowledge. In short, to all intelligent and deep students of the Upanishads, the term, as used here, carries an unsaid secret message: that the meditator should not overindulge either in the life of *mis*apprehensions or in those deep silent moments of pure meditations—the moments of *avabodha.* Krishna indicates that *sadhakas,* during their early practices, should not overindulge in the world of their perceptions nor try to practise too long and weary hours of meditation and force their inner silence.

In the same stanza, by two insignificant-looking words Krishna has conveyed to all generations of Geeta students an indication why *Yoga* is to be at all practised: 'It is capable of destroying all miseries.'

'When does one become a saint perfectly steadfast (Yukta)?'

यदा विनियतं चित्तमात्मन्येवावतिष्ठते ।
निःस्पृहः सर्वकामेभ्यो युक्त इत्युच्यते तदा ॥ १८ ॥

18. yadā viniyataṁ cittam
ātmany evā'vatiṣṭhate
niḥspṛhaḥ sarva-kāmebhyo
yukta ity ucyate tadā

यदा - When, विनियतम् - perfectly controlled, चित्तम् - mind, आत्मनि - in the Self, एव - only, अवतिष्ठते - rests, निःस्पृहः - free from longing, सर्वकामेभ्यः - from all (objects of) desires, युक्तः - united, इति - thus, उच्यते - is said, तदा - then.

---

*See Sámaiji's Discourses on Mandukya Upanishad: with Gaupada's Karika.

18. When the perfectly controlled mind rests in the Self only, free from longing for all (objects of) desires, then it is said that 'he is united' *(yuktah).*

This and the following five stanzas are a dissertation on the fruits of *Yoga,* and they explain what a perfect meditator can gain in life and what his experiences are while living in this world during and after his spiritual realisation. This section not merely provides the students with theoretical elucidations on the condition of self-integration and the status of Self-realisation, but it also very efficiently sharpens the enthusiasm in all true seekers who are ambitious to actually come to live the Truth explained therein. Very subtle truths, which are the intimate experiences of all meditators, are so beautifully hinted at in the exquisite suggestiveness of the language used in these verses.

Throughout in the Geeta, so far, Krishna has been stressing the necessity of one quality, steadfastness *(yuktah).* A complete and exhaustive definition has not been so far given to explain this crucial term. Although sufficient hints had been thrown here and there to indicate the nature of the man who is steadfast in devotion and *Yoga,* here we have almost a complete definition of it.

When the mind is completely under control, the stanza claims that it *'rests serenely in the Self alone'.* A little reflection can bring the truth of the statement to our easy comprehension. An uncontrolled mind is one which frantically gallops on, seeking for satisfaction among the sense-objects. We have been already told that the mind can be withdrawn from its preoccupations with its usual sense-objects only when it is firmly tied down to the contemplation of the Self which is the Eternal Substratum, the Conscious Principle that illumines all perceptions and experiences. Naturally therefore, a mind that is fully controlled is that which has lost itself, as it were, in the steady and continuous contemplation of the Self.

The above explanation is endorsed by the second line of the same stanza which gives us an inkling into the means by which we can fix our mind on the Supreme. *'Free from longing after all desires'* is the means that has been suggested repeatedly throughout the Lord's Song. It is unfortunate that the hasty commentators unconsciously come to over-emphasize the 'renunciation of all desires' as the cardinal virtue in Hinduism. There is an ocean of difference between the *'desires'* and the 'longing after desires'. Desires in themselves are not unhealthy, nor can they actually bring about any sorrow unto us. But the disproportionate amount of our clinging to our desires is the cancer of our mind that brings about all the mortal agonies into our life.

For example, desire for wealth is healthy inasmuch as it encourages the mind to act and to accomplish, to acquire and to save. But when this desire possesses an individual in such a way that he becomes almost hysterical with his own over anxiety at his very desire, it makes him incompetent to put forth any substantial creative. effort and thus accomplish glories worthwhile for the dignity of man.

A desire in itself cannot and does not bring about storms in the mind, as does our longing after those very same desires. The Geeta advises us only to renounce our *yearnings* for all objects of desires.

Through discrimination and proper intellectual evaluation of the sense-objects, when an individual has withdrawn his mind from its usual sense-gutters, the mind comes to take hold of the subtler and the divine theme of the Self for its contemplation. The limited and finite sense-objects agitate the mind, while the Unlimited and the Infinite Self brings peace and joy into it. This condition of sense-withdrawal and the entry into the Self of the mind is called its condition of steadfastness (*yuktah).*

'Such a Yogin's steadfast-mind is described below':

यथा दीपो निवातस्थो नेङ्गते सोपमा स्मृता ।
योगिनो यतचित्तस्य युञ्जतो योगमात्मनः ॥ १९ ॥

19. yathā dipo nivātastho
ne'ṅgate so'pamā smṛtā
yogino yata-cittasya
yuñjato yogam ātmanaḥ

यथा- as, दीपः- lamp, निवातस्थः- placed in a windless place, न - not, इङ्गते - flicker, सा- that, उपमा - simile, स्मृता - is thought, योगिनः- of the Yogi, यतचित्तस्य -of one with controlled mind, युञ्जतः- of the practising, योगम् -the Yoga, आत्मनः - of the self.

19. 'As a lamp placed in a windless place does not flicker', is a simile used to describe the *Yogi* of controlled mind, practising *Yoga* in the Self (or absorbed in the Yoga-of-the-Self.)

As an efficient complementary to the previous verse, this stanza explains the mind of the *Yogi* of collected thoughts who is abosorbed in

Yoga. This explanation is given through the help of a famous simile: as a lamp in a spot sheltered from the wind does not flicker'. The example is quite appropriate inasmuch as the mind is as fickle and unsteady as the tip of the flame. Thoughts appear in the mind at every second in a continuous stream, and these constant thought disturbances, each dying yielding place to a new one, give us the apprehension of a solid factor called the mind. Similarly, the tip of a flame also (it can be experimentally proved) is never steady, but the continuity of its change is so fast that it gives us an apparent llusion of solidarity.

When this flame is well protected from the fickle breeze, then it becomes steady in its upward flights. In the same fashion, the flame of the mind, flickering at the whims and fancies for the passing sensuous desires, when arrested in a meditator, becomes steadily brilliant, although the mind is made to contemplate upon the Self by a constant flow of *Brahmakara vritti.* In short, repeated and constant thought of *Brahman*—vast and infinite, eternal and blissful, the Sub-stratum for the entire universe—is the 'concentration in the Self' *(Yogamatmanah).*

'Having thus, through meditation, become single-pointed, what would be the stages of progress accomplished, is described here in the following four stanzas':

यत्रोपरमते चित्तं निरुद्धं योगसेवया ।
यत्र चैवात्मनाऽऽत्मानं पश्यन्नात्मनि तुष्यति ॥ २० ॥

20. yatro'paramate cittam
niruddham yoga-sevayā
yatra caivā'tmanā'tmānam
paśyann ātmani tuṣyati

यत्र - where, उपरमते - attains quietude, चित्तम - mind, निरुद्धम् - restrained, योगसेवया-by the practise of Yoga, यत्र -where, च - and एव -only, आत्मना - by the Self, आत्मानम् - the self, पश्यन् - seeing, आत्मनि - in the Self, तुष्यति - is satisfied.

20. When the mind, restrained by the practice of *yoga,* attains quietude, and when, seeing the Self by the self, he is satisfied in his own Self...

सुखमात्यन्तिकं यत्तद् बुद्धिग्राह्यमतीन्द्रियम् ।
वेत्ति यत्रनचैवायं स्थितश्चलति तत्त्वत: ॥ २१ ॥

21.sukham ātyantikaṁ yat tad
buddhi-grāhyam atīndriyam
vetti yatra na caivā'yam
sthitaś calati tattvataḥ

सुखम् - bliss, आत्यन्तिकम् - infinite, यत् - which, तत् - that, बुद्धिग्राह्यम् - that which can be grasped by reason, अतीन्द्रियम् - transcending the senses, वेत्ति - knows, यत्र - where, न - not, च - and, एव - even, अयम् - this, स्थित:- established, चलति - moves, तत्वत:- from the Reality.

21. When he (the *Yogi)* feels that Infinite Bliss—which can be grasped by the (pure) intellect and which transcends the senses, wherein established he never moves from the Reality...

यं लब्ध्वा चापरं लाभं मन्यते नाधिकं तत: ।
यस्मिन्स्थितो न दु:खेन गुरुणापि विचाल्यते ॥ २२ ॥

22. *yaṁ labdhvā cā'paraṁ lābhaṁ*
manyate na'dhikaṁ tataḥ
yasmin sthito na duḥkhena
gurunāpi vicālyate

यम् -which, लब्ध्वा -having obtained, च -and, अपरम् -other, लाभम् -gain, मन्यते – thinks, न - not, अधिकम् - greater, तत:- than that, यस्मिन् - in which, स्थित:- established, न -not, दु: खेन -by sorrow, गुरुणा - (by) heavy, अपि -even, विचाल्यते - is moved.

22. Which having obtained, he thinks there is no other superior to it; wherein established, he is not moved even by heavy sorrow.

तं विद्याद् दु:खसंयोगवियोगं योगसंज्ञितम् ।
स निश्चयेन योक्तव्यो योगोऽनिर्विण्णचेतसा ॥ २३ ॥

23.taṁ vidyād duḥkha-saṁyoga-
viyogam yoga-saṁjñitam
sa niścayena yoktavyo
yogo'nirviṇṇa-cetasā

तम् - that, विद्यात् - let (him) know, दुःखसंयोगवियोगम् - a state of severance from union with pain, योगसंज्ञितम् - called by the name of Yoga सः - that, निश्चयेन - with determination, योक्तव्यः - should be practised, योगः - Yoga, अनिर्विण्णचेतसा - with mind steady and undespairing.

23. Let that be known: the severance from the union-with-pain is *Yoga*. This *Yoga* should be practised with determination and with a mind steady and undespairing.

These four verses together give a complete picture of the state of *Yoga*, and Krishna ends them with a very powerful call to man that everyone should practise this *Yoga* of Meditation and self-development. In order to encourage man and make him walk this noble path of self-development and self-mastery, Bhagavan explains herein the goal that is gained by the meditator. When the mind is completely restrained, as explained in the above two stanzas, it attains to serene quietude, and in that slience it gains an experience of the Self, not as anything separate from itself, but as its own true nature.

This self-rediscovery of the mind to be itself in fact nothing other than the Divine Conscious Principle, is a state of Infinite Bliss, inasmuch as this awakening to the cognition of the Self can take place only when the individual-ego has smashed down its limiting adjuncts and has thereby transcended its identifications with the body, mind, and intellect.

That this Bliss is not an objective experience such as is gained during the pleasures of the world, is evidently indicated by the qualification that it 'transcends the senses' (*ati-indriya*). Ordinarily, we gain our experiences in the world outside through our sense-organs. If the spiritual masters' promise is that the Self-realisation is a state of bliss, we are ordinarily tempted to accept it as a goal, but when they say that it is beyond the senses, the seekers start feeling that the promises of religion are mere bluff. The stanza, therefore, has to insist clearly that this Bliss of Self-recognition is perceivable through the pure intellect.*

A doubt may arise now that, as a result of all these almost super-human efforts, when an individual has at last come to experience this Transcendental Bliss, it may provide only a flashy moment of intense living, which may then disappear, demanding all over again similar

———* **Intellect that is purified of its *rajoguna* and *tamoguna* is called in Vedanta the pure intellect. *Tamas* and *rajas* respectively create in man the 'veiling of Truth' (*avarana*) and the consequent agitations (*vikshepa*). When both of them are to a degree removed, to that degree the percentage of *sattva* increases in the intellect, and it is called the pure intellect. When an intellect comes under the influence of pure *sattva*, it ends in an experience of infinitetranquilitywhich is the nature of the Self, and the Self is experienced on thus transcending the intellect.**

superhuman efforts to rediscover one more similar moment of Bliss experience. To remove this possible misunderstanding., the stanza insists: *'established wherein he never departs from his Real state.'* The Geeta repeatedly endorses that the experience of the Self is an enduring state from which there is no return.

Even supposing one has gained this Infinite Bliss, will he not again come to all the sorrows that are natural to every worldly being? Will he not thereafter feel as much as anyone else the urge to strive and struggle, to earn and hoard, the thirst to love and get loved, etc? All these excitements which are the carbuncles upon the shoulders of an imperfect man are denied in a perfect one when the following stanza * explains the Supreme Truth as 'having come to which no one can consider any other gain as equal to it, much less ever anything greater.'

Even after all these explanations, the Lord Himself raises the question which a man of doubts may entertain. It will be quite natural for a student, who is striving to understand Vedanta purely through his intellect, to doubt as to whether the experience of Divinity can be maintained even during moments of stress and sorrow and in periods of misery and mourning. In other words, is not religion a mere luxury of the rich and the powerful, a superstitious satisfaction for the weak, a make-belief dream-heaven for the escapist? Can religion and its promised perfection stand unperturbed in all our challenges of life: bereavements, losses. disease, penury, starvation? This doubt—which is quite common in our times too—has been unequivocally answered here with a daring statement that *'wherein having established one is not moved even by the heaviest sorrow.'*

To summarise: by the quietude of the mind, gained through concentration, when one comes to rediscover one's own Self, his is the Bliss Absolute which through the senses cannot be preceived, † and yet, through a pure intellect** can be lived, and having reached which there is no more any return -having gained which there is no greater gain to strive for and which is not shaken even by the lashings of the greatest tragedies in our existence—is the wondrous Truth that has been indicated by the Geeta as the Self, the goal of all rational men of discrimination and spiritual aspirations.

---

* Stanza 22

† And therefore, not gross.

** Meaning, when the intellect has been transcended, since pure *sattva*intellect cannot maintain itself as a time-space-causality instrument.

This Self is to be known; and the means of knowing this goal, as well as the state of its experience, is called *Yoga* in Geeta.* Here we have one of the noblest, if revolutionary, definitions of *Yoga*.

We had earlier explained how Geeta is an incomparable restatement of the declarations of the Upanishads in the context of the Hindu world at the time of the Mahabharata. The old idea that *Yoga* is a strange phenomenon, too difficult for the ordinary man to practise or to come to experience, has been remodelled here into a more tolerant and divinely all-comprehensive definition. *Yoga,* which was till then a technique of religious self-perfection available only for a reserved few, has been made a public park into which everyone can enter at his freedom and entertain himself as best as he can. In this sense of the term, the Geeta has been rightly called a revolutionary Bible of Renaissance in Hinduism.†

Apart from the divine prerogative of an incarnation, we find a dash of revolutionary, zeal in Krishna's constitution, both in his emotions and character. And when such a divine revolt enters the field of culture and spirituality, He could not have given a more spectacular definition of *Yoga* than what He gives us here: 'Yoga—a state of disunion from every union-with-pain.' This reinterpretation of *Yoga* gives not only a striking definition of it, but it is couched in such a beautiful language of contradiction that it arrests the attention of the student and makes him think for himself.

The term *Yoga* means contact. Today, as it is, man in his imperfections has contacts with only the world of finite objects and, therefore, he ekes out of life only finite joys. These objects of the world are contacted through the instruments of man's body, mind, and intellect. Joy ended is the birth of sorrow. Therefore, life through the matter instruments is the life of pain-*Yoga(duhkhasam-yoga)*.

Detachment from the *Yoga* is naturally a process in which we disconnect *(viyoga)* ourselves from the fields of objects and their experiences. A total or even a partial divorce from the perception of the world-of-objects is not possible so long as we are using the mechanism of perceptions, the organs of feeling, and the instruments of thinking. To get ourselves detached from the mechanism of perceptions, feelings, and thought would naturally be the total detachment from the pain-*yoga*.

* Stanza 23.

† 'General Introduction', Chapter I.

Existence of the mind is through its attachment: the mind can never live without attaching itself to something. If it has to detach from one object, it is possible for the mind only when it has attached itself to another. For the mind, to detach from pain caused by the unreal is to attach itself to the bliss. That is the nature of the Real. In this sense, the true *Yoga,* which is seeking and establishing an enduring attachment with the Real, is gained only when the seeker cries a halt in his onward march towards pain and deliberately takes a 'right-about-turn' to proceed towards the Real and the Permanent in himself. This wonderful idea has been most expressively brought out in the phrase which Bhagvan gives here as a definition of *Yoga.*

A little scrutiny will clearly enable us to realise that, in defining *Yoga* thus, the Gopis' Lover has not introduced any new ideology into the stock of knowledge that was the traditional wealth of the Hindu scriptures. Till then *Yoga* was emphasized from the standpoint of its goal rather than from the explanation of its means. This over emphasis of the goal had frightened away the faithful followers from its salutary blessings, and the technique of *Yoga* became a secret boon meant only for a few.

Even true seekers thus got extremely frightened of our religion and Arjuna was one of them. To persuade him to come and play in the parlour of our religion is the missionary work that Krishna had to undertake in the Geeta. The missionary in Krishna could not have done it better than by explaining to Arjuna that *Yoga* is nothing but a 'renunciation of his contact with sorrows' and a direct entry into the halls of Bliss which is his own real nature. When we consider this definition of *Yoga* in this light, it is a surprise indeed that it has not become as famous as it should have been had the students of Geeta really grasped the infinite blessings of this inimitable explanation.

This is to be practised, insists Krishna, with an'eager and decisive mind'. To practise with firm resolve and an undespairing heart is the simple secret of the highest success in the practice of meditation, as the *Yoga* with the True is gained through a successful *viyoga* from the false.

If to be very near the fireplace is to feel uncomfortably warm, to get away from the fire is to reach the embrace of the cool and the comforting atmosphere. If to live among the finite objects and live its limited joys is sorrow, then to get away from them is to enter into the realm of Bliss which is the Self. This is *Yoga.*

'Further instruction regarding Yoga is now continued after the above short digression. Moreover...'

संकल्पप्रभवान् कामांस्त्यक्त्वा सर्वानशेषतः।
मनसैवेन्द्रियग्रामं विनियम्य समन्ततः ॥ २४ ॥

24. *saṁkalpa-prabhavān kāmāṁs*
tyaktvā sarvān aśeṣataḥ
manasaive' ndriya-grāmaṁ
viniyamya samantataḥ

संकल्पप्रभवान् - born of sankalpa (imagination), कामान् - desires, त्यक्त्वा - having abandoned, सर्वान् - all, अशेषतः– without reserve, मनसा - by the mind, एव - even, इन्द्रियग्रामम् - the whole group of senses, विनियम्य - completely restraining, समन्ततः - from all sides.

24. Abandoning without reserve all desires born of *sankalpa,* and completely restraining the whole group of senses by the mind from all sides...

शनैः शनैरुपरमेद् बुद्ध्या धृतिगृहीतया।
आत्मसंस्थं मनः कृत्वा न किंचिदपि चिन्तयेत ॥ २५ ॥

25. *śanaiḥ-śanair uparamed*
buddhyā dhṛti-gṛhītayā
ātma-saṁsthaṁ manaḥ kṛtvā
na kiñcid api cintayet

शनैः - gradually, शनैः - gradually, उपरमेत् - let him attain quietude, बुद्ध्या - by the intellect, धृतिगृहीतया - held in firmness, आत्मसंस्थम् - placed in the Self, मनः - the mind, कृत्वा - having made, न - not, किंचित् - anything, अपि - even, चिन्तयेत let him think.

25. Little by little, let him attain quietude by the intellect held in firmness; having made the mind established in the Self, let him not think of anything.

In the last section, the entire goal of *Yoga* was indicated as that state *'wherein the mind, through the practice of concentration, comes to get itself absolutely restrained,'* Later on, we were given a glorious word-picture of the state of enjoyment and perfection that one will be introduced to in this state of meditation. This theoretical exposition has no practical value unless exhaustive instructions are given as to how a diligent seeker can bring about this total mental poise consciously in a deliberate spiritual act of perfect self-control.

In these two brilliant stanzas the subtle art of meditation has been explained. The sacred secret as to how to bring the mind to a single pointedness and, thereafter, what we should do with that mind in concentraton and how we should approach the Truth and ultimately realise It in an act of deliberate and conscious becoming—are all exhaustively indicated in these two significant stanzas.

Renouncing 'all' *(sarvan)* desires 'fully' *(aseshatah)* by the mind, control all the sense-organs from their entire world of sense-objects. Herein every word demands commentary since every phrase leaves a hint which is so important in ultimately assuring for the seeker a complete success. It is not only sufficient that all desires are renounced, but each desire must be *totally* eradicated. By these two terms (*sarvan and aseshatah),* no trace of doubt is left in the minds of the seekers as to the condition of their mental equipoise during the moments of their higher meditation. The term *aseshatah* means that even the desire for this perfection in *Yoga* is to be in the end totally renounced.

'Renunciation of desires' is advised here with a very necessary and important qualification; but, unfortunately, the unintelligent had been ignoring in Hinduism this significant qualification, and had thus perverted our sacred religion to act and behave as though it recommended a life of indolence with neither any ambition to achieve nor any desire to accomplish. The term *'born of sankalpa'* is a very significant term, qualifying the desires that are to be renounced totally and fully. The term *'sankalpa'* had been already explained earlier* with reference to which we can easily understand that it is the renunciation of such agitation-breeding desires that is meant here.

When once this renunciation of the disturbing desires has been accomplished, the individual's mind gains strength and stamina to assert itself; at first to make the wild horses of the sense-organs more tame and work under greater control, and, soon, it comes to restrain all the sense-organs from all sense-objects, from all sides.

It is scientifically very true that our mind is not able to control our sense-organs, for it has been rendered weak and thoroughly impotent due to the permanent agitations caused by its own false desires. Once the

---

* Stanza 2.

mind gets strong as a result of its conquest over the desires, it discovers in itself all the strength and capacity to control the *indriyas* from all sides. This process of quietening the mind can never be accomplished in a hasty action, or by any imagination, or by any strange and mysterious method. It is clearly indicated by the very insistence that the Geeta makes in this stanza that the seeker should '*attain quietude as a result of his withdrawal from the world of sense-objects by degrees.*' Slowly and slowly (*sanaih-sanaih)* the mind gains more and more quietude.

No doubt, when the sense-organs have stopped their mad onrush among their respective objects, a certain amount of mental quietude is gained. The methods of intensifying this inner peace have been indicated in this stanza.*

'*Patiently, with the intellect, the mind is to be controlled and rested in the contemplation of the Self.*' This advice is extremely important to every seeker, and it gives the next item of the programme for a meditator when he has accomplished, through the exertion of the mind, a total withdrawal of himself from the sense-world during his meditation.

The mind that is thus brought to a relative quietude is next to be controlled by the subtler personality layer in the meditator, which is his intellect. Just as the senseorgans were controlled and restrained by the mind, the mind is now treated by the discriminating intellect and brought under complete restraint. Mind cannot be restrained except by fixing it to the exclusive contemplation of one idea. Mind, we have noticed, is but '*a thought flow*' and, as such, the constant thought of the Nature of the Self is the exercise by which the mind is restrained by the intellect. A mind that has merged in the steady contemplation of the Self becomes, as it were, still, and a divine quietude comes to pervade its very substance. This is, as it were, the last lap of the journey to which deliberate and conscious action (*purushartha)* can take any seeker.

Krishna's exhaustive theory, which can be practised by any sincere devotee concludes in these two stanzas with a warning as to what the seeker should avoid at this moment of inward silence and peace. The Lord here does not instruct the seeker on what he should positively do. The Divine Flute-player says: '*Let him not think of anything*', when he has reached this state of inward inner peace.

After the 'halt-moment'** there is nothing more for the seeker to act and achieve. All that he has to do is to avoid starting any new line of imagination. '*Undisturbed by any new thought wave, let him maintain*

* Stanza 25

** See Swamiji's Meditation and Life.

the inner silence and come to live it more and more deeply,' is all the instruction that the technique of meditation gives to the meditator. 'Knock, and thou shalt enter,' is the promise: the 'knocking' is done, and to the Supreme Presence thou shalt enter...erelong (*acirat).*

No two simple-looking stanzas any where in thespiritual literature of the world, including the books in Hinduism, can claim to have given such an exhaustive amount of useful instructions to a seeker as these two stanzas in the Geeta. Even in the entire bulk of the Divine Song itself, there is no other similar couple of stanzas which can stand a favourable comparison with this perfect pair.

As an instruction to those who have a fickle, unsteady mind, the following is added:

यतो यतो निश्चरति मनश्चञ्चलमस्थिरम् ।
ततस्ततो नियम्यैतदात्मन्येव वशं नयेत् ।। २६ ।।

26. yato-yato niścarati
manaś cañcalam asthiram
tatas-tato niyamyaitad
ātmany eva vaśam nayet

यत:- from whatever cause, निश्चरति - wanders away, मन:- mind, चञ्चलम् - restless, अस्थिरम् -unsteady, तत: तत: -from that, नियम्य -having restrained, एतत् -this, आत्मनि -in the Self, एव -alone, वशम् - (under) contrôl, नयेत् - let (him) bring.

26. From whatever cause the restless and the unsteady mind wanders away, from that let him restrain it, and bring it back to be under the control of the Self alone.

Every student who tries to understand the above two verses and put them into practice should necessarily come to despair at his own incapacity to control the mind and fix it constantly in the contemplation of the Self. In utter despair every seeker must come to realise that the mind irresistibly wanders away from its point of concentration because the mind is, by nature, restless (*chanchala)* and unsteady (*a-sthira).* It can neither constantly think of one object nor consistently think of the different objects. By these two terms qualifying the mind—restlessness and unsteadiness—Krishna has brought out a vivid and realistic picture of the entire mind as it is experienced by all true seekers striving on the path of meditation. These two phrases are so impressive that we shall find, later on, that Arjuna himself, while crystallising his doubts into language, uses them quite naturally.

Thus, during practice, even though the seeker has brought his sense-organs to a large extent under his control, still the mind, disturbed by the memories of its past experiences, would shoot out in search of its sense-objects. These are the moments of dejection and even despair for the seekers. These wanderings of the mind may be due to very many reasons: the memory of the past, the near presence of some tempting objects, the association of ideas, some attachment or aversion or, may be, even the very spiritual aspiration of the seeker. Lord Krishna's instruction here is very categorical and all-embracing. He says: '*whatever be the reason because of which the restless and the unsteady mind wanders away,*' the seeker is not to despair, but should understand that it is the nature of the mind to wander and that the very process of meditation is only a technique to stop this wandering.

'Let him bring it back': The seeker is advised to bring back the mind that has, as it were, rushed out into its own self-appointed dissimilar channels of thinking. This withdrawal of the mind may be successful to a degree by sheer willpower, but, as soon as it has reached the bosom, it will and it should rush out again into another fancied line of thinking. Very rarely the *sadhakas* realise that the mind means 'the flow of thought'. A steady, motionless mind is no mind at all. And, therefore, in the technique of meditation, when the mind is withdrawn from the sense-objects, this very process of withdrawal is to be complemented by a conscious effort on the part of the meditator in applying the same mind at once in the contemplation of the Self. This idea has been remarkably well brought out when the Lord complements his instruction by the term, *'bringing it under the sway of the Self alone'*.

'The following few stanzas explain the effect of the Yoga of Meditation upon its true practitioners':

प्रशान्तमनसं ह्येनं योगिनं सुखमुत्तमम् ।
उपैति शान्तरजसं ब्रह्मभूतमकल्मषम् ।। २७ ।।

27. praśānta-manasam hy enam
yoginam sukham uttamam
upaiti śānta-rajasam
brahma-bhūtam akalmaṣam

प्रशान्तमनसम् - one of peaceful mind, हि - verily, एनम् - this, योगिनम् - Yogi, सुखम् - bliss, उत्तमम् - supreme, उपैति - comes, शान्तरजसम - one whose passion is quietened, ब्रह्मभूतम् - Brahman become, अकल्मषम् - one who is free from Sin.

27. Supreme Bliss verily comes to this Yogi whose mind is quite paceful, whose passion is quietened, who is free from sin, and has become *Brahman.*

As we have just now indicated in the previous stanza, when an individiual's mind has been arrested from its agitated roamings in the world of objects, and fixed consistently upon the Self, by degrees the mind gathers more and more quietude and, ultimately, when the flow of thoughts cases, the mind also ends. Where the mind has ended, there the individual is awakened to the experience of the Infinite Nature of the Self. Naturally, the meditator (*Yogin) 'comes to the Supreme Bliss'.*

An intelligent enquirer has every right to question this assertion; for, in a true science the scientist has no right to assert at random his own opinion without arguments and to expect the students to gulp it all immediately down! In the second line of the verse are given reasons how the quietened mind is the open window through which the prospect of the Self comes to our view. A mind thus held steadily in the inner atmosphere of thrilled silence comes to drop off all its previous *vasanas:* the mind gets 'freed from taint' (*a-kalmasham).*

In Vedanta, technically, the impurities of the mind are called *mala,* and it is considered as constitued of the 'spiritual non-recognition, and the consequent 'mental agitations'. The 'veiling power' (*avarana)* generated by the inertia of the intellect (*tamas)*, creates in its wake the disturbing 'agitations' (*vikshepa)* in the mental zone. The agitation nuisance in the mind is most prominent when it is under the influence of the *rajoguna.* The Vedantic theory explaining 'the fall of man' to sorrow is fully echoed in the terms used by the Lord here: (a)'passions quietened' (*santa rajasam),* and (b) 'free from taint' (*a-kalmasham).*

An individual in whom all agitations have ceased and, consequently, who has become perfectly freed from his ignorance of the Reality, should naturally be considered as one who has regained his Knowledge of the Self. As long as there is agitation, so long there is the mind; and the Self identified with the mind is the ego—who was the seeker who started meditating—in the above process of meditation.

When, as it has been explained, the meditator has exposed his mind to the atmosphere of the inner peace and quietude, he comes to end completely all his mental agitations and, therefore, the ego rediscovers itself to be nothing other than the Self. This nondualistic Truth has been openly declared by the Lord through His brilliant phrase, 'Brahman-become' (*Brahmabhoota), in describing the man of Self-realisation.*

'Having thus explained the achievement of a true meditator'the Lord explains how this experience of the Self can be, thereafter, the constant life of the Perfect One':

युञ्जन्नेवं सदाऽऽत्मानं योगी विगतकल्मषः ।
सुखेन ब्रह्मसंस्पर्शमत्यन्तं सुखमश्नुते ॥ २८ ॥

28. *Yuñjann evam sadātmānam*
yogī vigata-kalmaṣaḥ
sukhena brahma-samsparśam
atyantam sukham aśnute

युञ्जन्-practising Yoga, एवम्-thus, सदा-always, आत्मानम्-the Self, योगी-Yogi, विगतकल्मषः-free from sin, सुखेन easily, ब्रह्मसंस्पर्शम्-caused by contact with Brahman, अत्यन्तम्-infinite, सुखम्-bliss, अश्नुते- enjoys.

28. The Yogi, always engaging the mind thus (in the practice of Yoga), freed from sins, easily enjoys the Infinite Bliss of 'Brahman-contact.'

Engaging himself thus in the battle for evolution and the consequent inward mastery, a true meditator steadily grows out of the shadowy regions of his own spiritual ignorance and imperfections to smile forth in luxurious extravagance into the sparkling shine of Knowledge. When the meditator keeps his mind undisturbed in the roaring silence within, in the brilliant whitehead of meditation, his mind gets purified like a piece of iron in the smithy's furnace. In short, as we said earlier and elsewhere *, the 'halt-moment' is the last possible frontier liine upto which human effort can raise the mind.

There it ends itself, just as a balloon, as it goes higher and higher, blasts itself in the rarified atmosphere of the higher altitudes, dropping itself down and merging the ballon-space with the space in the altitude.

* Read Swamiji's *Meditation and Life.*

Similarly, the mind too, at the pinnacle of its meditation, shatters itself, drops down leaving the ego, and merges with the Supreme. Just as the space in the balloon automatically and naturally merges with the space outside when once the balloon is exploded, so too, when the finite mind is ended, '*with ease it attains the Infinite Bliss arising out of its contact with Brahman.*'

The term 'contact' here has served as a convenient handle for the dualists to argue that the Lord is indicating thereby the existence of the Truth-principle as separate from the Truth-seeker. Obviously, this is absurd. The argument of the dualists can be acceptable only if we can afford to forget the definition of the term *Brahman*. In the Hindu scriptures *Brahman* is the all-pervading Reality, which is limited by nothing, † and therefore, we cannot have a knower-of-*Brahman* (or a feller-of-*Brahman)*, who has a separate existence, to come in *contact* with *Brahman* and enjoy the Bliss. It can only mean, if a consistent sense is to be read in the scriptures, that the individual seeker *becomes Brahman* and comes to experience the Infinite Beatitude which is the essence of Truth.

Krishna here is trying to make an agitated, restless, inquisitive intellect understand the positive and dynamic Reality which can and shall be gained when the mind and intellect are transcended. *Had he said the seeker will become happiness,* Arjuna would have hesitated in accepting it, believing that in the Self there is no positive joy. To make his unprepared intellect **perceive** the experienceable joy of the Infinite, the Divine Cowherd has to borrow a vivid phrase from our ordinary life, and so He says that the meditator '*attains the Infinite Bliss through the Brahman-contact.*' This phrase '*Brahman-contact*' should be understood as 'Self-contact' —a usage in contrast to the finite joys which we gain ordinarily in life through the 'not-Self-contact.'

In the following stanzas we get a description of the effects of Yoga and the consequent perception of oneness in the pluralistic world'

सर्वभूतस्थमात्मानं सर्वभूतानि चात्मनि ।
ईक्षते योगयुक्तात्मा सर्वत्र समदर्शनः ॥ २९ ॥

29. *sarva-bhūtastham ātmānam*
sarva-bhūtāni cātmani
īkṣate yoga-yuktātmā
sarvatra sama-darśanaḥ

* See Swamiji's *Discourses on Isavasya Upanishad,* especially stanzas 1, 4, and 5.

सर्वभूतस्थम्-abiding in all beings, आत्मानम्-the Self, सर्वभूतानि- all beings, च- and, आत्मनि- in the Self, ईक्षते -sees, योगयुक्तात्मा- one who is harmonised by Yoga, सर्वत्र- everywhere, समदर्शन:- one who sees the same everywhere.

29. With the mind harmonised by Yoga he sees the Self abiding in all beings and all beings in the Self; he sees the same everywhere.

All religions in the world are great, but, indeed, none of them is so perfect as the religion of the Hindus, if by religion we mean the science of self-perfection. In this stanza, the author of the Geeta says in unequivocal terms that the perfect man of Self-knowledge or God-realisation is not merely one who has realised his own divinity, but is also one who has equally understood and has come to live in an intimate knowledge and experience of the Divinity inherent in all creatures without any distinction whatsoever. The Awareness in us is the Awareness everywhere, in all forms and names, and this Divine Awareness is the very essence in the entire world of perceptions and experiences. To contact the Infinite in us is to contact the Eternal everywhere.

To a true man of realisation in Hinduism there is no more a world to be addressed, even if it be in divine compassion, by the disgusting phrase, 'O! Ye Children of Sin'; like Ramtirtha, a Hindu saint of Perfection, cannot but address the entire living kingdom, 'O! Ye Children of light.'* This idea of the consummate revelation of 'God —I am', gained by the meditator, is the peak of Perfection, endorsed and aimed at by the Hindu seers. This idea has been most effectively brought out in this stanza.

This pluralistic phenomenon as a manifestation of and a projection on the Immortal Truth, is very well brought out in almost all the preceding chapters. Thus, the essence in all names and forms is the same transcendental Self. Just as the mud in all mud-pots, the gold in all ornaments, the ocean in all waves, the electricity in all bulbs, the Self is the Essence and the Substratum in the world-of-objects.

From the physical body we perceive the physical world, and from our emotional level we perceive the emotions in others. So too, from our intellectual level alone can we intelligently contact the ideas working in other intellects. As it has been asserted in the previous chapter, when an individual transcends himself beyond his intellect he comes to rediscover his own Divine Nature, and from that Spiritual Centre, when he

* Or address them as 'My own Self in the form of ladies and gentlemen.'

looks out, he finds the Self to be pervading everywhere. The Self can cognise only the Self everywhere. The meditator, on transcending his intellect, *becomes the Self;* and to the Self there is nothing but the Self everywhere. To the mud, there are no pots; to the gold, there are no ornaments.

With this understanding in our mind, the stanza becomes quite clear when it says : *'He beholds the Self in all beings and equally beholds all beings in the Self.'* Such a Perfect One, who has realised the actual unity in the world of diversity, alone can afford to entertain the equality of vision in all circumstances and conditions—on a noble Brahmin, a cow, an elephant, a dog, and a pariah. †.

'Now will be described the effect of this perception of unity of the Self':

यो मां पश्यति सर्वत्र सर्वं च मयि पश्यति ।
तस्याहं न प्रणश्यामि स च मे न प्रणश्यति ।। ३० ।।

30. yo mām paśyati sarvatra
sarvam ca mayi paśyati
tasyāham na praṇaśyāmi
sa ca me na pranaśyati

य: -who, माम्-me, पश्यति-sees, सर्वत्र-- everywhere, सर्वम्-all, च-and, मयि- in me, पश्यति-sees, तस्य of him, अहम्- I, न-not, प्रणश्यामि-vanish, स: -he, च-and, मे-to me, न-not, प्रणश्यति-vanishes.

30. He who sees Me everywhere, and sees everything in Me, he never gets separated from Me, nor do I get separated from him.

Earlier we were told that, on reaching his goal, the meditator *'attains Infinite Bliss of the Brahman-contact.'* * We explained therein that the term 'contact' indicates, by a kindly suggestion, only the nondual Reality which is the theme of all the Upanishads. Here, in this stanza, we have Krishna's own commentary upon that term used in a couple of earlier stanzas. Once having awakened to the Self, the Perfect Master thereafter recognises every where nothing but the Self.

'He who sees Me in all things and sees all things in Me': In this stanza, as everywhere else, the first person singular 'I' and 'Me' is to be

† Chapter V, 18.

* Stansa 28.

understood as the Self. On re-reading the stanza in the light of this annotation, this stanza and the previous one together express more fully the pregnant meaning of one of the most famous Upanishadic declarations found in the *Isavasya.* * The second line of the Geeta-verse now under review is almost a commentary upon the last word in the *Upanishad mantra* referred above. (*Na-vijugupsate).*

'He never becomes separated from Me': On transcending the intellect, the experience of the ego is not that it sees or preceives or cognises the Eternal, but the ego rediscovers itself to be, in its essence, nothing but Self (*Sivoham).* The dreamer, on awakening, himself becomes a waker, a dreamer can never see or recognise the waker as separate from himself.

'Nor do I become separate from him': The dualists are rather shy to accept that Infinite Divinity is their real nature, for, they are, as ego-centres, conscious of their own bodily vanities and sins. In no clearer term can we more exhaustively describe the unadulterated Truth of the essential divinity in man. Lord Krishna, here, is in no way trying to conceal his meaning that a meditator, when he has fulfilled the process of detachment from the not-Self, himself *becomes* the Eternal and the Infinite. It may be a staggering truth but, all the same, it is the Truth. Those who are hesitating and wavering may well do so and continue disbelieving their own divine potentialities. But the intimate experience of the long hierarchy of *gurus* in India and the mystic saints all over the world endorse this unbelievably plain truth that, in essence, 'the Self in an individual is the Self everywhere.'

At present there is a divorce of ourselves from ourselves; the ego is a rebel who has exiled himself from his native kingdom, the Self. On rediscovery of the Self, the ego *becomes* the Self in such a happy blending of a homegeneous whole that, thereafter, there is no distinction between the ego and the Self. On awakening, the dreamer becomes the waker; not only does the dreamer become the waker, but the waker can never remain separate from the dreamer. In ordinary divorces, either party can divorce the other, and yet the divorced can still maintain an emotional relationship with the one who had separated and gone away. Here, the Lord says that not only the seeker comes to feel the Self-hood, but I, the Self, becomes homogeneously one with Him.

* Read Swamiji's *Discourses on Isavasya Upanishad, Mantra 4.*

In fact, once we understand that 'a misguided God is man,' it becomes amply clear that, rightly guided, man rediscovers himself to be nothing other than the Supreme. An actor playing the part of a beggar can never really be a beggar, and the moment he drops down the part he plays, he becomes what he was in the past. In reality, even while he was playing the role, he was not a beggar. This daring declaration of Vedanta, in itself, is not at all difficult to understand, but the deluded feel terribly aghast at this revelation and, in their own imperfections, they refuse to believe this truth. They have not the guts to take the responsibilities of living the godly life. Krishna's courageous statement in this stanza leaves no pinhole for any doubt to enter on this sacred conclusion of all the scriptures of the world, espectially of the immortal Upanishads.

Emphasising the same idea that the man of perfect self-control and meditation, on realising his Self, 'becomes the Self, the following is added:

सर्वभूतस्थितं यो मां भजत्येकत्वमास्थितः ।
सर्वथा वर्तमानोऽपि स योगी मयि वर्तते ॥ ३१ ॥

31. sarva-bhūta-sthitam yo mām
bhajaty ekatvam āsthitah
sarvathā vartamāno'pi
sa yogī mayi vartate

सर्वभूतस्थितम्-abiding in all beings, यः-who, माम्-me, भजति-worships, एकत्वम्-in unity, आस्थितः -established, सर्वथा-in every way, वर्तमानः -remaining, अपि-clso, सः-that, योगी-yogi, मयि-in me, वर्तते-abides.

31. He who, being established in unity, worships Me—who dwells in all beings, that Yogi abides in Me, whatever be his mode of living.

The meditator who has integrated himself into a single-pointedness, steadily contemplates (*bhajati*) upon me, the Self, which is the essential Spark of Life in all forms in the world. Such an individual, whatever be his activities in the external world, ever lives in 'Me' through a conscious awareness of the Self. This stanza is given here mainly to indicate that a Man of Realisation need not necessarily retire to some secret cave in some forgotten valley of the Himalayas, but can maintain his Divine Consciousness in all states of existence, in all conditions of life, and under all happy or unhappy circumstances. When a man is ill, no doubt, he has to withdraw himself from the fields of activities, strains, and recreations, and go to a sanatorium in order that he may revive. Having regained the maximum natural health, the patient need not, thereafter, live for ever in the sanatorium, but, on the other hand, he can come back to the old fields and live, perhaps, a more active life than even before.

Similarly, a distintegrated man of unhealthy temperaments is, in spiritual life, treated through meditation, and when he regains his godly strength and vitality, he can certainly re-enter the fields of his earlier games and yet maintain in himself the cultural perfections and the spiritual knowledge that he had gained during his spiritual treatment.

It was only a mischievous misunderstanding, deliberately brought into the traditional thought by the saboteurs of our culture, that had perverted the noble Hindu idealism. There is a very unhealthy tendency among us to believe and preach that spiritual Self-realisation is a death-knell to all activities. Had it been true, we would not have been discussing now this very textbook which is the noble labour of a Man of Realisation, Vyasa, reporting the wisdom of the Divine Personality. Work, in fact, can be performed and really enduring fruits gained only when the worker has got himself established in the Self. The labour of the Geeta is to advise Arjuna that work is a means of self-development.

In the same Geeta there is a deeper significance that Krishna, the Perfect, is also on the battlefield, exposing himself, perhaps more, to the dangers of the battle than prince Arjuna himself. A charioteer meets the arrows earlier than the warrior who stands behind him! To enter such a battlefield, armed with nothing but his irresistible smile and, in effect, becoming himself almost the uncrowned Lord of the battlefield, wherein the entire war unconsciously comes to revolve round Krishna himself, the central personality—this means that a Man of Realisation, in all conditions, will be able to enter into any activity and still maintain in himself the unbroken awareness of the Divine that he is.

Reading this commentary some students might feel that we are bringing an overemphasis in our over-enthusiasm. We can only request them to ponder for themselves the all-comprehensiveness of the words used in the daring statement: 'Whatever his mode of life be (*sarvatha-vartamanopi)*, the meditator (*Yogin)* abides in Me.'

आत्मौपम्येन सर्वत्र समं पश्यति योऽर्जुन ।
सुखं वा यदि वा दु:खं स योगी परमो मत: ॥ ३२ ॥

32 ātmaupamyena sarvatra
samam paśyati yo'rjuna
sukham vā yadi vā duḥkham
sa yogī paramo mataḥ

आत्मौपम्येन-through the likeness (similarity) of the Self, सर्वत्र-everywhere, समम्-equality, पश्यति-sees, यः- who, अर्जुन-O Arjuna, सुखम्-pleasure, वा-and, यदि-if, वा-or, दुःखम्-pain, सः -he, योगी-Yogi, परमः -highest, मतः - is regarded.

> 32. He who, through the likeness (sameness) of the Self, O Arjuna, sees equality everywhere, be it pleasure or pain, he is regarded as the highest *Yogi.*

True meditators, well established in their intellectual understanding and spiritual experience, recognise intuitively the Divine Presence immanent in everything. Such men of Perfection see in all activities the glory of the Self and understand their own bodily functions as nothing but the grace of the Self. For them, there is no experience but the Divine. Everything experienced in the gross world and the subtle realm within, is nothing but an emanation from the Eternal Self. It is a pity that such an obvious stanza, in the most sacred scripture of the Hindus, is so carelessly overlooked by our *pundits.*

The educated class has come to glorify the philosophy of simpler scriptures in the world because the priests in them are intelligent enough to emphasize the fundamental social rules which their religion insists upon. Of all religions in the world, Hinduism alone is neglecting to emphasize the scriptural quotations which prescribe our social duty and laws of communal living. Here is a stanza which, in the midst of a disquisition upon the highest philosophical truth, declares the individual's duty towards others in the society. In its elaborate implications this stanza is an exhaustive commentary upon the primary Biblical instruction: 'Love thy neighbour as thyself'.

The highest *Yogi,* according to the Geeta, is one who feels the pains and joys of others as intimately as if they were his own. The famous ethical rule: 'Do unto others as you would be done by', in itself, is a most unpleasant instruction to every ordinary man because, in his selfishness, he is easily tempted to ask why after all, should he consider others as himself? The uninitiated would naturally be tempted to follow the unethical ways of life in his instinctive selfishness.

The previous few stanzas explained why one should love one's neighbours. The *Yogi,* after his experience of the Self, comes to recognise the whole world as himself, and whether one should love or not one's own right leg is no problem at all for anyone in the world. All the limbs and parts of one's body are equally sacred to an individual because one can easily experience one's own intimate identity with all the different parts of the body. If your tongue were to be unconsciously bitten by your own teeth, you will never think of punishing the teeth for the crime they have done; for, both in the tongue and the teeth you pervade equally. Once having realised the Self, when I come to feel everywhere the presence of Me as the Self, the whole universe of names and forms becomes for Me the one integrated form in which, at all places and at all times, 'I alone AM.'

Such an inidividual, who has in his realisation come to feel the entire universe as his own form, is called a true *Yogi* by the Singer of the Geeta. In short, a seer of Self-realisation instinctively becomes a divinely compassionate man producing more in the society than what he will therein consume, and creating in the community much more than what he destroys during his lifetime. Love is his very breath; kindness his very sustenance.

In thus concluding the description of perfect *Yogi* with a word-picture of the perfect man's attitude to life and his relationship with the world outside, no doubt the eagerly listening student gets extermely fascinated. But the practical man-of-the-world in Arjuna immediately discovers his incapacity to attain the goal pointed out here, and, therefore, the Pandava prince raises his own doubts in the form of a question.

'Seeing that the Yoga described—the Yoga of Right Knowledge—is very difficult to attain, Arjuna wishes to know the surest means of gaining this Yoga':

अर्जुन उवाच

योऽयं योगस्त्वया प्रोक्तः साम्येन मधुसूदन ।
एतस्याहं न पश्यामि चञ्चलत्वात्स्थितिं स्थिराम् ॥ ३३ ॥

Arjuna uvāca

33. *yo'yam yogas tvayā proktah*
sāmyena madhusūdana
etasyāham na paśyāmi
cañcalatvāt sthitim sthirām

यः - which, अयम्- this, योगः - Yoga, त्वया-by thee, प्रोक्तः - taught, साम्येन- by equanimity, मधुसूदन-O slayer of Madhu, एतस्य- its, अहम्-I, न-not, पश्यामि- see, चञ्चलत्वात्- from restlessness, स्थितिम्-continuance, स्थिराम्-steady.

Arjuna said

33. This Yoga of Equanimity, taught by Thee, O Slayer of Madhu, I see not its enduring continuity because of the restlessness (of the mind).

The most practical-minded Aryan that he was, Arjuna, the man of action, could not at all be moved by the mere poetic beauty of any ideology. He was thirsty to live and, therefore, the abovementioned philosophy of meditation and successful victory over the cravings of the flesh could not charm him away to any idle humour. He shot point blank very realistic questions to explode the seemingly impracticable philosophy that had been explained in this chapter.

'Detachment from pain-attachments' (*duhkha-samyoga-viyoga)* was the definition of *Yogi* that the originality in Krishna could provide in this chapter. The process of achieving a substantial success in this 'Detachment-*Yoga'* has been explained herein as the technique of withdrawing the mind from the objects by lifting it to the planes of higher contemplations. The theory is that a redeemed mind, when it comes to a single-pointed devotion in the contemplation of the Self, becomes stilled, and ends its egocentric pilgrimage through the ignorance of the Truth and the consequent misjudgement of the world.

The goal pointed out—perfect equanimity in all conditions, challenges, and circumstances of life—is, no doubt, an admirable gain, but the technique seems to be a sheer poetic fantasy which has no roots on the soils of the realistic actualities of life. The acute— though gross— intellect of Arjuna, systematically approaching the science of Self-realisation, discovers, as it were, a dangerous missing link in the chain of its arguments. Mercilessly, the man of war is hammering at this weak point with almost a sure confidence that he will expose immediately the hollowness of Krishna's philosophy.

Thus Arjuna tauntingly points out that *'this Yoga which you have been teaching me',* which has been indicated by the mental tranquility, is not at all practicable. the argument given out by Arjuna and the daring with which he directly faces his teacher, show the characteristic spirit of a true student of Vedanta. Blind faith can give no entry into the fields of pure spititualism. The teachers are to answer and clear all the doubts of the seekers. But, in questioning the philosophy exponded by a teacher, the students must indicate the logical arguments by which they had come to feel the particular weakness in that philosophy. Here Arjuna gives all his arguments to show why the state of evenness of mind is a dream as long as the human mind is, by nature, 'restless' in its own agitations.

Even in thus contradicting the philosophy, Arjuna is extermely careful. He does not say that the mental equanimity cannot be at all gained through meditation. But his doubt is that it cannot be an experience of *'long endurance'*. The implication is that, even if after years of practice the mind were to be won over, the experience of the Self can only be momentary. And although a full'experience' of the Infinite can be had in that split-moment,this direct realisation cannot be maintained by the Man of Knowledge for any length of time because the mind is, by nature, essentially ever restless.

It is quite interesting how a receptive student like Arjuna gathers unto himself the style and language, the vocabularly and diction of his teacher. The terms qualifying the mind, used here by Arjuna, are terms that have been borrowed from the Lord's own declaration earlier.*

As if making himself more clear to his teacher, Arjuna adds the following stanza which, in fact, takes the edge off the spearhead of his logic in the previous stanza.

चञ्चलं हि मन; कृष्ण प्रमाथि बलवद् दृढम् ।
तस्याहं निग्रहं मन्ये वायोरिव सुदुष्करम् ॥ ३४ ॥

34. cañcalam hi manaḥ kṛṣṇa
pramāthi balavad dṛḍham
tasyāham nigraham manye
vāyor iva suduṣkaram

चञ्चलम्-restless, हि-verily, मनः - the mind, कृष्ण- O Krishna, प्रमाथि- turbulent, बलवत्-strong, दृढम- unyielding, तस्य-of it, अहम्-I, निग्रहम्-control, मन्ये-think, वायोः - of the wind, इव-as, सुदुष्करम्- difficult to do.

34. The mind verily is O Krishna, restless, turbulent, strong, and unyielding; I deem it quite (as) difficult to control as the wind.

* Stanza 26: 'Manas-chanchalam-**asthiram**'

There is an atmosphere of intimacy and love, surrender and respect in the very note of helplessness in Arjuna's words in this stanza. This art of making an emotion echo through the Rhythm of the words is often met with in Sanskrit, although rarely, if ever at all, we see them in English poetry also.*

There is an ocean of difference between a modern man condemning the sacred scriptures of our land and a true seeker questioning the same philosophy in his honest attempt to understand the full import and the wealth of suggestiveness contained therein. In his acute awareness, Arjuna, as it were, realises deep within himself his own subjective experience that a mind cannot be stilled—as it is ever *'turbulent, strong, and unyielding'*.

These three terms are quite pregnant with their own imports. Turbulency shows not only the speed in the flow of thoughts but also their restlessness and agitations, causing on the surface uneven waves rising pell-mell. Not only that the flood of thoughts flow fast and rough, but having reached its destination of some sense-object or the other, it gets itself so powerfully attached to it that it becomes strong in its new roots. Mind in turbulence is, no doubt difficult to arrest; when it gets strongly riveted, it is difficult to pluck it away from its attachments; and the third characteristic feature of the mind is that, when it has flown into any channel of its own choice, for the moment it is so *'unyielding'* that it is impossible for the individual to pull it back from its flight and persuade it to stay at the determined point of concentration. It is to be remembered that this was the technique advised by Krishna for the practice of meditation earlier in this chapter.—

The strength and vigour, the vivacity and treachery, the penetrativeness and all-pervasiveness of the mind cannot be better expressed than by the simile given here: *'as that of the wind'* In raising this question, Arjuna is asking Krishna some practical tips by which he can gain a perfect control over the stormy nature of *'the unyielding, strong, turbulent, and restless mind'*. Herein, unlike in the previous stanza.** the Lord is addressed by his most familiar term, 'Krishna', a word that comes from the root *krish,* meaning, 'to scrape'. The term Krishna is applicable to the Self because, on realization of the True, the delusory threats of the mind and the consequent dreamy *vasanas* will all be scraped from our cognition.

* The curfew tolls the knell of parting day'.— Grey's Elegy.

— Stanza 26.

** Wherein He was addressed as 'the destroyer of the demon, Madhusudana'.

The bloody hands of the dreamer get automatically cleaned and all the moral stigma attached to the murder completely falls off when he wakes up. Similarly, the mind and its onslaughts, its *vasanas* and their tyranny, the intellect and its quest, the physical body and its appetites... all, all end with the rediscovery of the true nature of the Self. Therefore, the poet-philosopher Vyasa, in his immortal classic, the *Mahabharata*, paints the inner Self as Lord 'Krishna', the Flute-bearer of Brindavan. In Sanskrit this is aspecial art, unknown to any other language in the world: using a proper noun to indicate the peculiar quality of the person that is to be suggested in the context of the narration.

Accepting the arguments of Arjuna, the Lord answers to prove that there is a method by which the invincible mind can be brought under control.

श्रीभगवानुवाच
असंशयं महाबाहो मनो दुर्निग्रहं चलम् ।
अभ्यासेन तु कौन्तेय वैराग्येण च गृह्यते ॥ ३५ ॥

Sri Bhagavān uvāca
35. asamśayam mahābāho
mano durnigraham calam
abhyāsena tu kaunteya
vairāgyeṇa ca gṛhyate

असंशयम्- undoubtedly, महाबाहो- O mighty-armed, मनः - the mind, दुर्निग्रहम् - difficult to control, चलम्- restless, अभ्यासेन-by practice, तु-but, कौन्तेय-O Son of Kunti, वैराग्येण-by dispassion, च-and, गृह्यते- is restrained.

The Blessed Lord said

35. Undoubtedly, O mightly-armed, the mind is difficult to control and is restless; but, by practice, O Son of Kunti, and by dispassion it is restrained.

Vyasa, the immortal dramatist, in his preoccupation with the philosophical explanations, does not for a moment drop down the mantle of poetry off his shoulders. This is, in fact, the incomparable glory of the poet-philosopher Vyasa. Indeed, there is a bustling moment of dramatic possibility at this point in the Geeta, which an hasty artist overlook; but not Vyasa. And, in fact, it is such artistic moments fulfilled so magnanimously, that give Geeta the compelling charm of a magic even to those who do not understand it at all!

Krishna knew his Arjuna: the warrior, the man of action, the daring adventurer, and the ruthless realist. When such a tumultuous personality

spurs himself out with a drawn dagger to agree to and condemn the noble philosophy of a true missionary, the teacher must have the balance of mind to approach the rebel-intellect with divine understanding and extreme tact. At this juncture, in the Geeta, the situation, to put it in a nutshell, is this: the Lord propounds a theory that 'mind stilled is Self gained', and Arjuna argues that mind cannot be stilled and so Self cannot be gained.

Both of them are arguing upon the possibility or otherwise of realising the Self in the subtle kingdom within, and, therefore, therein no objective demonstration is ever possible. In the material sciences of the world, all arguments between scientists can be finally determined and completely proved on the laboratory tables and on graph-papers. But, in the case of the subjective science, it being a transaction between two equally integrated personalities, arguments as such, though unavoidable, must be very carefully directed. And he is a true missionary who is a master of the psychology of his opponent. Conversion of another's intellect into the right channels is no rough act of any woodcutter or any grave-digger; it is the hard but careful art of cutting jewels: he is to shape the heart of another and bring out of it more light.

When an Arjuna-like man gets hold of an idea in all enthusiasm, the best technique is to yield to him. 'Stoop to conquer' is the secret of success in perversions natural in the ignorant. Thus, the great psychologist, Krishna, with the very first word in his reply, quietly disarms his mighty adversary, and immediately tickles the vanity of the warrior with the term, 'no doubt, O mighty-armed'. Krishna admits that the mind is turbulent, strong, unyielding, and restless and that it is very difficult to control, and therefore, the goal of perfect and enduring tranquillity cannot be *easily* achieved.

By this admission Arjuna is flattered; all the more he is mentally brought to a restful peace by being reminded that he is a mighty -armed soldier in life. The taunting implication in it is obvious: to achieve the impossible and the difficult is the job of the mighty-armed; it is no glory for a warrior to claim that he plucked half-a-dozen flowers from a bush in his own courtyard. The mind is, no doubt, a great enemy; but, the greater the nobler also is the victory.

In the second line of this stanza, again, the eternal missionary in Krishna very carefully weighs his words and uses the most appropriate terms to soothe the mind of Arjuna. *'O Son of Kunti, it can be brought under control'*, is an assertion which comes only as the last word in the entire stanza. Through practice and renunciation the mind can be brought under reins in the beginning, and ultimately to a perfect 'halt — this is the confident, reassuring declaration of the Lord in the Geeta.

Renunciation has been already described earlier in the Geeta as *sannyasa*, which was defined as renunciation of (a) all clinging attachments to the objects of the world, and (b) lingering expectations of the fruits of action. These two are the main causes for the agitation of thoughts which again thickens the flood of the thoughtflow and makes the mind uncontrollable. As Sankara describes it, 'practice' *(abhyasa)* is 'constant' repetition of the same idea regarding one and the same object-of-thought.'* This consistency of thought during steady meditation generally gets diverted and dissipated because of the frequent explosive eruptions of desires. Whipped by new desires that are rising at every moment, the thoughts wander into dissimilar channels of activities, upsetting the inner equilibrium and thereby shattering the true vitality of the inner personality.

Thus viewed, practice *(abhyasa)*. strengthens renuciation, and detachment *(vairagya)* deepens meditation Hand in hand, each strengthening the other, the progress is maintained.

In scriptural textbooks the arrangement of words is to be carefully noted, for, in all cases, the words are arranged in a descending order of importance. To every seeker the question comes at one time or the other: whether he should wait for the spirit of detachment to voluntarily arrive in his mind, or he should start his practice. The majority wait in vain for the accidental moment of *vairagya* before they start their *abhyasa*. The Geeta, in this stanza, clearly declares that such an expectation is as ridiculous as waiting for the harvest of crops for which we never sowed the seeds!

Let us analyse life, question its experiences, argue with ourselves, and note carefully how much we put into life and how much we gain from life as a return. When we become aware of the deficit balance each time, we, of necessity, shall start enquiring how our life can be more profitably reorganised so that our entire coffers of joy and happiness can be replenished to their brim. Soon, the study of the Sastras will follow, which will give us an inkling into the wonders of the moral life, the wisdom of the ethical values, the joys of self-control,the thrills of growth, and the suffocation of the egocentric little-life.

* Read Swamiji's *Meditation and Life.*

From the moment we are trying to become aware of our own lives, we are in the realm of 'practice' *(abhyasa)*. As a result of this, the detachment that comes to us automatically is the true and the enduring 'detachment' *(vairagya)*. All else is a sham show of stupid self-denial which cramps a human soul and distorts and perverts his intelligence into an ugly figure riddled with its own hysterical ravings and bleeding with its own psychological ulcers. *Vairagya* born out of abhyasa alone is the charter for free spiritual growth: of your own accord never renounce anything. Let your attachments with things, of their own accord, drop off as a result of your intellectual growth into the higher planes of better understanding and truer estimation of things and beings, happenings and behaviours, occurrences and incidents around you in life. When, through right 'practice', enduring 'detachnent' has come rushing in full gush into our inner lives, then the mind comes under our control because it has no more any world of pluralistic objects to roam in, and the only world where it has a free access is the world of equanimity and sameness.*

'What then will be the lot of those who have no self-control?'

असंयतात्मना योगो दुष्प्राप इति मे मतिः ।
वश्यात्मना तु यतता शक्योऽवाप्तुमुपायतः ॥ ३६ ॥

36. *asamyatātmanā yogo*
duṣprāpa iti me matiḥ
vaśyātmana tu yatata
śakyo'vāptum upāyataḥ

असंयतात्मना-by a man of uncontrolled self, योग: - Yoga, दुष्प्राप: - hard to attain, इति-thus, मे-my, मति: -opinion, वश्यात्मना -by the self controlled one, तु-but, यतता-by the striving one, शक्य: -possible, अवाप्तुम्-to obtain, उपायत: - by (proper) means.

36. Yoga, I think, is hard to be attained by one of uncontrolled self; but the self-controlled, striving, can obtain it by (proper) means.

In the previous stanza extreme emphasis was placed on practice. But what constitutes the spiritual *(abhyasa)* was not indicated even indirectly in that verse. A scientific book that leaves missing links, either in its arguments or in its logic, is no textbook at all. In the stanza under review Krishna is giving a direct clue to what he meant by the term *abhyasa*.

---

* Chapter V, 19; Chapter VI, 32.

Though the Lord's statement expresses quite an obvious truth, even a divine master like Krishna dare not declare in Hinduism any statement of his own with the authority of a scriptural text. At best, any interpreter of religion can only declare his opinion. All intelligent men and serious students of the scriptures have the right to entertain their own individual opinions, conclusions, and convictions based upon logic and personal experiences. But these opinions can change, and they do keep on changing from time to time inasmuch as they depend entirely upon the conditions of the times and the types of minds that come to evaluate and declare these opinions. In Sanskrit the term *matam* means 'opinion'. The conclusions or opinions of Christ, Mohamed, Krishna, Buddha, and others became religions seemingly different from one another. But all of them have the same fundamental truths which constitute what they term in Sanskrit as *dharma*.

As his personal opinion, the Divine Singer of the Geeta declares here that the uncontrolled and, therefore, a totally dissipated personality cannot bring into the pursuit of religion the necessary amount of dynamic vigour and vitality to sustain him till he reaches the peak of his Self-rediscovery. It is therefore said: '*Yoga is hard to be attained by one of uncontrolled Self*.

An individual who barters himself to slave among the sense-objects according to the mad dictates of his flesh, or one who dances to the death-tunes sung by his voluptuous mind, or one who roams about endlessly to fulfil the tyrannical orders of a drunken intellect—such an one has no peace of mind nor the strength of sustained aspiration to goad him on towards the Temple of truth within himself.

So long as the sense-organs are not properly controlled, 'the agitations of the mind' cannot be pacified. An agitated mind is no instrument, either for listening or for reflection or for meditation—and without these three, the 'veiling power' cannot be rolled up The agitations (*vikshepa)* and veiling (*avarana)* are caused by 'activity' (*rajas)* and 'inactivity' *(tamas)*; and we have already found that without controlling these two temperaments, the 'unactivity' (*sattva)* cannot predominate in the seeker.*

It is natural in all discussions that we generally present our own arguments against a team of opposite arguments so that the discrimina-

* See 'Fall and Rise of Man' in Swamiji's *Discourses on Kenopanishad.*

tive intellect of the listener may, by contrast, come easily to judge the acceptability and reasonableness of our own viewpoint. Krishna uses here this commonplace technique of every drawingroom when he, in the second line, explains, as a contrast, how '*the self-controlled, striving hard by right means, can obtain It.*' Self-control, achieved through the process of a total withdrawal of the sense-organs from their respective objects, is no doubt, the beginning of the spiritual life.

Even in ordinary life, when we want to achieve something solid, the man-of-the-world will have to live, to a large extent, in self-denial. The life of a candidate during the election time, of a student before his examinations, of an actor or a dancer before his first reception.. are all examples wherein we find that the individuals deny themselves all their idle preoccupations in their own anxiety to win their success in their respective fields. If for material gains and flimsy ephemeral glories we have to deny ourselves in order to acquire and possess the desirable, how much more should we deny ourselves the joys of the world outside in order to win the glories of the eternal and the permanent, the infinite and the absolute Bliss of the Self?

Not only is it sufficient that the seeker is seemingly denying himself all the sense-objects, though this seems to be the most general misunderstanding among almost all sincere seekers in India today. In the name of religion or spiritual practice, they, at least for some years, seem to live in self-denial and self-punishments, shamelessly insulting themselves and carelessly persecuting their own physical urges and even biological needs. This sort of a devilish and suicidal self-codemning tyranny over oneself always ends in an outburst of satanic forces from the very seeker.

We do not find in such dull-witted practitioners any blossoming of their spiritual fragrance but, on the other hand, we see them metamorphosed into monsters who are, at best, a scandal even to the worst of civilisations known in history! Many of the modern educated men point out to such damaged instances and declare that religion only wrecks human life and that it can add no beauty to the personality! They can be considered as wise in their judgement only in an age when we start accepting that cooking is dangerous because a few cooks get their fingers burnt in the kitchen!

Lest the student of the Geeta also should fall a prey to such a misunderstood and misconceived spiritualism,Bhagavan indicates here that the self-controlled seeker can, by '*striving rightly, obtain It.*' Not going to the cinemas and not visiting the playgrounds and are in themselves assurances that the students will pass their examinations. The time wasted in such merrymaking must be properly utilised in intelligent study, which alone can vouchsafe for them a success in their examinations. Here too, if a student appearing for an examination in mathematics were to read the whole night his geography textbooks, he may not thereby assure for himself any glorious success; he must strive rightly in order that he may gain the true success.

Similarly, when a seeker has, through self-control, conserved in himself energies which would otherwise have got dissipated in the gutters of sensuality, he must know how to direct those energies through the right channels whereby he can get himself detached from his misconceived self-projections and ultimately realise for himself his own Self-hood. That such an intelligent seeker *'can obtain It'* is the optimistic philosophy of this ever smiling God of the Hindus, Lord Krishna.

With these two verses, Krishna exhaustively answers the question raised by Arjuna, and what follows clearly indicates that the Pandava prince has been convinced by the Lord's reply.

The question yet remains, what would be the lot of one, 'self-controlled, and striving hard through right means', who could not yet fulfil and reach the goal?

अर्जुन उवाच

अयतिः श्रद्धयोपेतो योगाच्चलितमानसः ।
अप्राप्य योगसंसिद्धिं कां गतिं कृष्ण गच्छति ॥ ३७ ॥

37. *ayatiḥ śradhayo'peto*
yogāc calita-mānasaḥ
aprāpya yoga-samsiddhim
kām gatim kṛṣṇa gacchati

अयतिः - uncontrolled, श्रद्धया- by faith, उपेतः - possessed, योगात्-from Yoga, चलितमानसः - one whose mind wanders away, अप्राप्य-not having attained, योगसंसिद्धिम्- perfection in Yoga, काम्- which, गतिम्-end, कृष्ण- O Krishna, गच्छति -meets.

37. He who, though possessed of faith, is unable to control himself, whose mind wanders away from Yoga, to what end does he, having failed to attain perfection in Yoga, go, O Krishna?

In these and the following two stanzas Veda Vyasa makes Arjuna raise a pertinent question, so that Krishna may get yet another chance to bring right under the footlight the supremely optimistic philosophy of Vedanta. None striving on the Path Divine can ever be destroyed; and whatever he accomplishes will be faithfully carried over as a legacy for the individualised self in its pursuit here or in the hereafter. Each today is an added link in the endless chain of dead-and-gone yesterdays. The lengthening chain continues growing by adding to itself, link after link, all the yesterdays. Death is only one of the incidents in a human existence, and the tomorrow has no accidental or arbitrary beginning but it is only a perfect continuation of the today.

Carefully voicing forth his vague doubt, Arjuna asks as to what will happen to one who strives with *sraddha* but fails to accomplish complete self-control during his lifetime, or, due to lack of sufficient self-control falls from *Yoga?* The idea is that such an individual may thereby come to lose both the little joys of the sense-objects and the Absolute Bliss in the hereafter. The Vedantins, even while they condemn the mere life of sense-objects, do not, even for a moment, deny the fact that there are traces of joy in the sense-life also. According to them, daring thinkers as they were, the joys of the sense-objects (*vishaya ananda)* are, in their essence, nothing other than glimpses of the Spiritual Bliss (*Brahmananda).* The secret import of the question is that those who faithfully follow Krishna's theory may come to lose both the chances of experiencing the finite and the Infinite joy.

Such a seeker, striving all his life to live in self-control, will be a conscious escapist—avoiding all the finie joy-temptations in the gross world here. But, if the uncertain factor called death were to creep in to clip the thread of his life with the scissors of time, he will be losing his chances of gaining the Absolute Beatitude which is the goal that Lord Krishna seems to point out in his Divine Song. Again supposing the seeker, due to lack of self-control, falls from *Yoga?* To win in *Yoga,* no doubt, is a great victory; a gain *par excellence.* But if, in the race, one were to get knocked down by the stealthy club of sensuousness, he stands to lose both here and hereafter. Naturally, Arjuna wants some reassurances from Krishna as to what will happen to such an individual.

In this stanza also we must note very carefully that the term *sraddha* is not some maddening superstition which encourages a blind faith. According to Sankara, *sraddha* is the right intellectual apprehension of the deeper imports and the fuller significances of what the teachers teach and the scriptures declare.* The inspired devotion that springs up in a bosom, from among its solid intellectual convictions gained through a true appreciation, is the mighty power called faith 'that can move mountains' and 'bring the very heavens to the earth'.

To throw more colour onto the picture of the spiritual desperado whom Arjuna has attempted to paint in the previous stanza, the following is added:

कच्चिन्नोभयविभ्रष्टश्छिन्नाभ्रमिव नश्यति ।
अप्रतिष्ठो महाबाहो विमूढो ब्रह्मणः पथि ॥ ३८ ॥

38. kaccin no'bhaya-vibhraṣṭaś
chinnābhram iva naśyati
apratiṣṭho mahābāho
vimūḍho brahmaṇaḥ pathi

कच्चित्-is it that? न-not, उभयविभ्रष्टः - fallen from both, छिन्नम्-rent, अभ्रम्-cloud, इव-like, नश्यति-perishes, अप्रतिष्ठः -supportless, महाबाहो- o mighty-armed, विमूढः - deluded, ब्रह्मणः - of Brahman, पथि-in the path.

38. Fallen from both, does he not, O mighty-armed, perish like a rent cloud, supportless, and deluded in the path of Brahman?

Emphasizing in more elaborate terms the doubt already expressed earlier, Arjuna now enquires as to what happens to that seeker who, though striving hard with faith, but for want of restraint, falls from *Yoga* and thus fails to carry his efforts to the point of complete success. Will his efforts be baulked both here and hereafter? *'Fallen away from both'* is a very suggestive term which can be applied also to both the spiritual paths so far described: Knowledge and Action.

A sincere wayfarer, faithfully treading the path of self-control to rediscover the Self, may get lost if death were to rob him on his way or, for want of complete self-control, he were to fall from the *Yoga.* The striking example with which this idea is being brought out by Arjuna is one of the most brilliant poetic strokes in the entire Geeta. This is often quoted in literary circles whenever an attempt is made to evaluate Vyasa, the poet, in Sanskrit literature.

In summer, mushroom-shaped floating castles of clouds raise themselves from behind the mountains to peep into the valleys below. At

* Read Swamiji's Talks on Sankara's Viveka choodamani.

the touch of some strong current of wind the mass takes to flight, leaving along its trail small bits of fleecy cloudlets. These little ones, torn away from the parental bulk, get knocked about and are at the mercy of every wandering breeze. Such summer cloudlets, aimlessly kicked about according to the whims and fancies of the winds, can never fulfil the expectations of the farmers or the clamour of the thirsty. Not fulfilling themselves, they get tossed hither and thither without any haven for themselves. '*Like the rent cloud*', Arjuna asks, 'will not the aspiring self in the seeker be forced to roam about and ultimately get lost in the vast amphitheatre of the universe?'

'Why does Arjuna ask this question?'

एतन्मे संशयं कृष्ण छेत्तुमर्हस्यशेषत: ।
त्वदन्य: संशयस्यास्य छेत्ता न ह्युपपद्यते ॥ ३९ ॥

39. etan me samsayam kṛṣṇa
chettum arhasy aśeṣataḥ
tvad-anyaḥ samśayasyāsya
chettā na hy upapadyate

एतत्-this, मे-my, संशयम्-doubt, कृष्ण-O Krishna, छेत्तुम्-to dispel, अर्हसि-ought to, अशेषत: - completely, त्वत्-than you, अन्य: - another, संशयस्य- of doubt, अस्य-of this, छेत्ता-dispeller, न-not, हि-verily, उपपद्यते-is fit.

39. This doubt of mine, O Krishna, please dispel completely; because, it is not possible for anyone but you to dispel this doubt.

In this concluding verse of this section, Arjuna frankly asks: *'This doubt of mine, O Krishna, you should completely dispel.'* The 'Eternal Scraper', Lord Krishna, alone has the Pure Wisdom that can rub out this doubt and quieten the agitations caused by it in the bosom of Arjuna. With this, his quetion, it becomes amply clear that his previous doubt has been totally dispelled. The earlier doubt was that 'Self-realisation is impossible since the mind, which is ever turbulent, can never be stilled.' The reply of the Lord has soothed out the knotty frill in Arjuna's mind.

Every true seeker, if he be diligent enough, must come to discover a couple of new doubts where a previously existing doubt has been cleared. The process of slowly eliminating all these doubts is the process of *vichara* that is practised both consciously and unconsciously during all *satsangs.*

The glorious life of the hereafter assured to every evolver, is classified hereunder on the basis of the intensity of the mental attitude and the spiritual in each one of them.

श्रीभगवानुवाच
पार्थ नैवेह नामुत्र विनाशस्तस्य विद्यते ।
न हि कल्याणकृत्कश्चिद् दुर्गतिं तात गच्छति ॥ ४० ॥

Sri Bhagavān uvāca
40. *pārtha naive'ha nāmutra*
vināśas tasya vidyate
na hi kalyāṇakṛt kaścid
durgatim tāta gacchati

पार्थ-O Partha, न-not, एव-verily, इह-here, न-not, अमुत्र-in the next world, विनाश: -destruction, तस्य -of him, विद्यते -is, न -not, हि -verily, कल्याणकृत् -he who does good, कश्चित्-anyone, दुर्गतिम्-bad state of grief, तात-O my son, गच्छति-goes.

The Blessed Lord said

40. O Partha, neither in this world nor in the next world is there destruction for him; none, verily, who strives to do good, O my son, ever comes to grief.

In the following five stanzas Bhagavan tries to explain the path of progress of a seeker whose spiritual endeavours have been either clipped by an untimely death or arrested by the intervention of some sensuous temptation. At the very opening of this section Krishna assures, with all the emphasis at his command, that *'neither here nor in the hereafter is there for him any destruction, who peforms the right action.'*

This statement is not a mere emotional assurance built upon some blind faith or a godly declaration that is to be swallowed down by the faithful without a wink because they are the sacred words that have come from the lips of a prophet. The Hindus do not accept any divine prerogative even for their gods, by which they can bypass the individual intellect and the rules of logic. Religion is a 'science of life', and it must explain completely the why and the wherefore of its practices.

Obedient to this incomparable trait in our culture, Krishna supports his statement with the philosophical truth: *Never for the doer of good, dear son, a woeful end.'* The one who acts rightly in the present can come to no grief in the future because, the future is but a product of the present and the good is that which yields but success and joy in the future.

The fear of Arjuna that the unsuccessful *Yogin*—a seeker obstructed and got held up on the path—will get lost *'as a rent cloud'* here and in the hereafter, has risen from his failure to appreciate the logical continuity and the perfect sequence that is ever in life. To consider that death is the end of an existence starting with the accident of birth, is a philosophy too rudimentary to be considered as complete and exhaustive. In fact, it is only with a stretch of the imagination that we can consider such theory as a philosophy.

Daring intellects, bravely pushing ahead in the quest to understand and comprehend the laws of life and the meaning and purpose of the universe, cannot but accept that the existence of an individual in its present embodiment is but a single pearl in the necklace of infinite beauty adorning the bosom of Truth. The present is the product of the past, and thought by thought, action by action, knowledge by knowledge we ourselves are creating the blueprint for our own future. Therefore, the Hindus believe in previous lives as well as in future births, otherwise called the theory of reincarnation. Based upon this principle Krishna insists that no seeker is ever lost, although he may slip and fall, or even end his present manifestation; tomorrow is but today continued.

The brilliant Lord of laughter and joy, Krishna, is the fittest mouthpiece to declare the Philosophy of Bliss, which is Vedanta. Never can we find a more optimistic note of hope and cheer in any philosophy in the world as in the Hindu view-of-life. And the Geeta, the Bible of the Hindus, truly portrays amidst peals of its thundering joys its celestial message of hope to mankind. In the entire length of the Geeta, nowhere else can we find such a complete assurance of hope as in the secod line of this stanza: *'The doer of good, O my son, never comes to grief.'*

In addressing Arjuna as *'O my son'*, Krishna here is not only following the traditional vocabulary of the Upanishads, but there is a deeper significance. A father, however deceitful, cunning, and cruel a brute he may be to everyone else in the world, cannot ever come to advise his own son a false philosophy. With a fatherly love, the man of wisdom in Krishna is assuring Arjuna that one who is striving in the direction of evolution shall never come to suffer any real fall. On the ladder of cultural growth, each step that is placed forward is an ascent towards the Absolute Perfection.

What exactly would be the destiny of a man who could not complete his pilgrimage in Yoga?' What then happens to him?'

प्राप्य पुण्यकृतां लोकानुषित्वा शाश्वती: समा: ।
शुचीनां श्रीमतां गेहे योगभ्रष्टोऽभिजायते ॥ ४१ ॥

41. prāpya puṇyakṛtām lokān
uṣitvā śāśvatīḥ samāḥ
śucīnām śrīmatām gehe
yogabhraṣṭo 'bhijāyate

प्राप्य-having attained, पुण्यकृताम्-of the rightous, लोकान्-worlds, उषित्वा-having dwelt, शाश्वती: -everlasting, : समा: -years, शुचीनाम्-of the pure, श्रीमताम्- of the wealthy, गेहे- in the house, योगभ्रष्ट: -one fallen from Yoga, अभिजायते-is born.

41. Having attained to the worlds of the righteous and having dwelt there for everlasting (long) years, he who had fallen from Yoga is born again in the house of the pure and the wealthy.

The hereafter is ordered by the actions performed and the motives entertained here. Actions in life can be mainly classified as *good* and *evil;* and the pursuers of evil can only slip down the path of evolution: Those who are doing good work alone can start their climb onto the higher points on the tower of their spiritual progress. Even here, our textbooks make a careful distinction and classify all good activities under two main headings: *(a)* actions performed with desires, and *(b)* those that are performed in a spirit of dedicated love and worship. Since reactions to our actions depend entirely upon the motives that propel our actions, the results accrued from selfish and selfess activities must necessarily differ among themselves. Naturally, there must be different routes of progress to the same pinnacle of perfection. All of them are being indicated here in the different stanzas of this section.

Those who have been living here, employing themselves in worship of the Lord with desire for heavenly enjoyments, shall be, after their death, reaching those planes of consciousness and, having exhausted their desires therein, they will be taking their births again here in the world '*in the houses of the pure and the prosperous*'. In short, all burning desires of every human creature will be fulfilled at one time or the other if the desire is strong enough and if it is not divorced from intense activities appropriate to their fulfilment.

But what happens to those who are pursuing the good in a spirit of selfless dedication?

अथवा योगिनामेव कुले भवति धीमताम् ।
एतद्धि दुर्लभतरं लोके जन्म यदीदृशम् ॥ ४२ ॥

42. athavā yogināṁ eva
kule bhavati dhīmatām
etaddhi durlabhataram
loke janma yadīdṛśam

अथवा-or, योगिनाम्-of Yogis, एव-even, कुले-in the family, भवति-is born, धीमताम्-of the wise, एतत् this, हि-verily, दुर्लभतरम्- very difficult, लोके- in the world, जन्म- birth, यत्- which, ईदृशम्- like this.

42. Or, he is even born in the family of the wise Yogis; verily, a birth like this is very dificult to obtain in this world.

The other type, which makes a direct and immediate manifestation, in which the continuity of the past is clearly noticeable, is the theme of this stanza. Those who are pursuing selfless *upasanas* thereby gain more and more their inner integration and, as a result of it, become dynamic minds capable of the highest meditaiton. The more integrated a personality is, the more spiritual he becomes and, therefore, he must be given a chance to fulfil himself, not in heaven which is a plane for enjoyment, but he must arrive right here to strive more diligently and achieve the highest. Such an ego-centre *(jeeva)*, as soon as it leaves one embodiment, immediately comes to manifest itself in a conducive atmosphere where it can continue its pilgrimage without any obstruction. It being an aspiring heart, it should necessarily come to be '*born only in a family of wise men of meditation*'.

This theory gives a lot of insight into the present-day fallacy which gives such an exaggerated importance to the unhealthy environments and makes everyone protest against their surroundings. No doubt, man is a creature of his environments; but the same, when viewed through the glasses of philosophy, gives also an insight into the fact that the individuals, in their own freedom, had ordered in the past their own present environments. By merely changing his environments, the individual concerned cannot progress; a habitual drunkard may still continue drinking on the sly even if he were to be brought into a dry city to live among teetotallers.

Examples like Sankara, Christ, the Buddha, and other great masters can be considered as supporting this philosophical theory. Such men of brilliant genius who, from their very early youth, exhibit superhuman knowledge and godly wisdom are, no doubt, rare. Krishna himself accepts here that such persons are '*very rare to obtain in this world.*' If the previous stanza explained the rebirth of an ego (*jeeva*) after an interval of existence in the heavens, this stanza explains the lives of the few who, after departing from one embodiment, immediately arrive in this world to continue their pilgrimage to Perfection.

'After reaching such conducive and helpful environments, will the fallen Yogi of the last life continue his spiritual life?' Listen:

तत्र तं बुद्धिसंयोगं लभते पौर्वदेहिकम् ।
यतते च ततो भूयः संसिद्धौ कुरुनन्दन ॥ ४३ ॥

43. tatra tam buddhi-samyogam
labhate paurva-dehikam
yatate ca tato bhūyaḥ
samsiddhau kurunandana

तत्र-there, तम्-that, बुद्धिसंयोगं-union with knowledge, लभते-obtains, पौर्वदेहिकम्-acquired in his former body, यतते-strives, च-and, ततः - than that, भूयः - more, संसिद्धौ- for perfection, कुरुनन्दन -O Son of the Kurus.

43. There he comes to be united with the knowledge acquired in his former body and strives more than before for Perfection, O Son of the Kurus.

It may be feared that an individual who is thus born again will have to start in his studies and practices all over again. To remove any such doubt, Krishna here explains that such an individual in his new life, under the conducive circumstances, gets naturally '*united with the intelligence acquired in his former body*'. Such a born *Yogi* completes his education much more easily than others since to him, it is not an education that is needed, but only a rivision or a recapitulation. In a very short time he discovers that all knowledge is bubbling up from within himself and to him study is but a rediscovery of a digested knowledge which was already lying dormant in him.

Not only that he comes to discover in himself the knowledge that he learnt in the past, but he easily finds in himself the required enthusiasm and energy for consistent self-application and vigorous pursuit. Knowledge without practice is a dull, dreary load upon the shoulders of a seeker. Krishna here assures that one '*fallen from Yoga*' in the past, when reborn in the right atmosphere, not only gains all knowledge easily, but comes to '*strive more than before for perfection,* O *Son of the Kurus.*'

Here again, Arjuna is addressed by such a loving term which particularly makes him remember that he himself is born in the noble family of the *Kurus* as a result of his own meritorious past. Perhaps, the Lord himself had to declare the Geeta directly to Arjuna because the past in his divine actions demanded such an experience.*

How can one get 'united with the intelligence acquired in his former embodiment?' Listen:

पूर्वाभ्यासेन तेनैव ह्रियते ह्यवशोऽपि सः ।
जिज्ञासुरपि योगस्य शब्द ब्रह्मातिवर्तते ॥ ४४ ॥

44. pūrvābhyāsena tenaiva
hriyate hy avaśo' pi saḥ
jijñāsur api yogasya
śabda-brahmātivartate

पूर्वाभ्यासेन-former practice, तेन-by that, एव-verily, ह्रियते-is born, हि-indeed, अवशः - helpless, अपि-even, सः -he, जिज्ञासुः - he who wishes to know Yoga, अपि -even, योगस्य-of yoga, शब्दब्रह्म-word -Brahman, अतिवर्तते goes beyond.

44. By that very former practice he is borne on in spite of himself. Even he who merely wishes to know Yoga goes beyond the *Sabdabrahman.*

At any given moment, our bank balance can only be the balance in our own credit-and-debit statement of accounts. No banker can give us more, nor can he cheat us with a less amount. Almost in the same fashion, in the cultural growth of a given mind and intellect, no God can either take any or give some, but can only hand over for each one of us our own exact balance. Each life has a logical continuity with its own past, as strictly as we experience in the day-to-day life that today is but an extension of yesterday. With this law of life in the mind, if we were to read the stanza, it becomes quite clear.

---

* It is clear from the *Mahabharata* that, as Nara and Narayan, Arjuna and Krishna had in the past performed severe *tapas* for a long number of years in the Badrinath peaks.

An individual who had been in *Yoga* in his past will be, *'by that very former practice, borne on in spite of himself'*. This is true even in our life here. An educated man, *in spite of himself,* will be carried away in his behaviour and conversation to exhibit his cultivated mental and physical habits. No cultured man can successfully imitate the idiot for a long time; so too, no rascal can with profit act the part of the noble for any length of time. Both will, sooner or later, be compelled, *in spite of themselves,* to exhibit unconsciously their true nature through their words, ideas, and actions.

Similarly, a man who had in the past lived the life of self-control, study, and practice gathers unto himself those cultural traits, and he, in this life, *'in spite of himself'* and in spite of all his adverse circumstances, environments, and conditions of life, cannot but instinctively come to exhibit—in his attitudes to life and in his behaviour towards the things and beings of the world— a tranquillty, a balance, which is a surprise ever to himself.

This is no mere theory. The truth of the statement is amply evident everywhere in any society, in all strata of its life, in all professions and in all departments of its activities. Each one of us has an instinctive bent of mind, and we are irresistibly drawn towards it *in spite of ourselves.* This pull is most powerful when they are essentially the evolutionary tendencies. Even a bandit chieftain can overnight turn himself himself into a determined seeker and erelong become the first great poet of the land, as Valmiki did in the past. Hundreds of such examples can be noted in our recent history and even amidst us today. In all these cases, the only satisfactory explanation will be that the individual mind-and-intellect is expressing through its given physical structure its own characteristic tendencies which it had acquired by itself in its past incarnations through its own wilful actions performed and deliberate motives entertained.

When an individual who was a fallen *Yogi* in the past is reborn, *'in spite of himself'* he is drawn towards a life of meditation and quietude a life of seeking and striving, a life of self-control and discipline. May he be put on the throne of a kingdom, or in the bustle of a marketplace, or in the ignominy of the gutters, he cannot but express his nobility of heart and the philosophical bent of his mind. All the wealth of the world commanded, unquestioned might and power gained, love or respect given, cannot persuade him away from his Path Divine. And, if the whole world stands surprised at his peculiar tendencies, we cannot at any time say that he himself is not of those who is gazing on with the wildest surprise and the uttermost amazement! *'By that previous practice alone is he borne on in spite of himself'*.

After observing this philosophical truth, Lord Krishna is naturally tempted to express the glory of meditation *(Yoga)* He says: *'One who has even the desire to know control (Yogi), he passes beyond the Vedic ritual'*. According to Sankara, the term *'Sabdabrahman'* used here denotes the words in the Veda, wherein the term *Veda* denotes only the ritualistic portion. Therefore the *Acharya,* commenting upon this portion, says that such an individual goes beyond all the charms for the promised fruits of the Vedic rituals. This may be considered, rightly, as a commentary rather too laboured, although its implications are indeed only too true. One who has warped his mind in the practice of self-control, study, and meditation in the past could not have any more fascination for the material wealth or the sensuous life, however celestial they may be. Even if this interpretation has thus a bearing on the context, we must admit that the term has been laboured by the Teacher of the *Advaita* philosophy.

In the tradition of the Upanishads, *Sabdabrahman* is expounded as the sacred mantra, OM*. This interpretation seems to fall in line with the traditional Hindu scriptures. In short, in the context of the discourses, † the Lord wants to glorify the Path of Meditation more than the Path of Action and Worship and, therefore, He says herein: *'Even the enquirer in the Path of Meditation goes beyond the finite fruits of worshipping OM, the Sabdabrahman.'*

'How is the Path of Meditation nobler than all others?' Listen:

प्रयत्नाद्यतमानस्तु योगी संशुद्धकिल्बिषः
अनेक जन्मसंसिद्धस्ततो याति परां गतिम् ॥ ४५ ॥

45. prayatnād yatamānas tu
yogi samśudhka-kilbiṣaḥ
aneka-janma-samsiddhas
tato yāti parām gatim

प्रयत्नात् - with assiduity, **यतमानः** - striving, **तु** - but, **योगी** - the Yogi, **संशुद्धकिल्बिषः** - purified from sins, **अनेकजन्मसंसिद्धः** - perfected through many births, **ततः** - then, **यतिः**- reaches, **पराम्** - the highest, **गतिम्** - path.

* 'Passing beyond this, men disappear in the Supreme, the soundless, unmanifest Brahman'— *Maitri Upanishad, VI—22.*

✓ The discourse of Krishna in this chapter is called 'Yoga of Meditation.'

45. But the *Yogi* who strives with assiduity, purified from sins and perfected (gradually) through many births, then attains the highest goal.

As we have been noticing till now, the mind-and-intellect of an individual functions through its body in the world outside as per the traits chalked out upon it by its past actions performed in its earlier lives. These channels of thinking, dug along the fields of the mind, determine the direction of its thoughts and the texture of its actions in the present. These lacerations on the subtle body are called in Vedanta as'sins', or as the 'dirt of the within'. These impurities are removed and the existing ulcers healed through selfless action.*

But even then, while reforming the wrong, negative tendencies of the mind, the individual will have to plough the fields of his mind with new patterns representing the constructive, divine tendencies. The meritorious *vasanas* (*Punya*) also can provide a man of meditation with severe obstructions. After having purified his mind of its unethical and sensuous tendencies, the aspirant practises meditation, and during the still moments of the peaceful peace in the depth of his depths, when he exposes his mind to the thrilled atmosphere of its vibrant silence,the noble traits also get completely wiped off. A mind thus rendered completely impressionless (*vasana*-less) is the end of the mind; since the mind is nothing but a bundle of *vasanas.* Where the mind has ended, there the ego has also ended, having *'then reached the highest goal'* or its Self-rediscovery.

The explanation of this theory would not perhaps be in print more than half a page but, in actually carving it out into our individual life, it may be the programme of very many lives' consistent practice.*'Through many births'* is a phrase often used by the honest Scientists of Life, the Rishis, in the Upanishads; and they are perfectly right; for, the evolution, as we all know, is not a drama of an afternoon, but is a slowly revealing history of progress through endless aeons.

Unfortunately, the clumsy pundit-class in our recent times has learnt to misuse such phrases—especially after the '*Pauranic*-era' and the '*Chaitanaya-age*'-in our sacred Bible to frighten away the Hindus from the sacred Hindu fold. According to the ill-read priests '*the many births*' are to be counted from the *present existence;* and their opinion

---

* See 'General Introduction', Chapter 1.

would have been certainly acceptable if we, at present, are all but members of the vegetable kingdom or mere unicellular non-entities. Even when he can read the scriptures with the intelligence and common sense of an average human being, if a pundit were to accept himself to be but a worm, surely we must accept his theory—of course, as applicable only to him. But we, with our intellects so fully developed, our minds so energetic and vigorous, our understanding so acute and sharp, cannot but feel confident that we have exhausted almost all the number of births that are indicated in the term *'through many births'.*

To one who has got the temperament to seek Life, the anxiety to realise the Perfection, the vigilance to understand the hollowness of the sense-life, the daring to follow the narrow footprints of the seers of the world, the appetite for infinite peace and tranquillity, the courage to live the moral and the ethical values, the bravery to barter one's all to achieve the higher....such an one is not a mineral man, not a vegetable specimen, not a member of the cattle world, but he is the noblest creation under the sun, standing right in front of the doors of Truth, demanding his admission into the *sanctum sanctorum!*

Right now in this very life is our last birth if we have a taste to meditate, an urge to seek, a daring to live the Life Divine.

There can be nothing which may sound as original as in this interpretation, to all diligent students of the Geeta. A sacred textbook that had been roaring, time and again, in an irrepressible spirit of optimism the message of hope and cheer with no threats of hell and brimstone anywhere in it, cannot be considered to have changed its music all of a sudden to declare that man has hopes of a salvation only after *'many births'* and not *'now and here'.* Even though this misinterpretation may perhaps be helpful to the saboteurs of our religion, no intelligent student of the Geeta can ever for a moment be hoodwinked by such false notes.

'Therefore'....

तपस्विभ्योऽधिको योगी ज्ञानिभ्योऽपि मतोऽधिकः ।
कर्मिभ्यश्चाधिको योगी तस्माद्योगी भवार्जुन ॥ ४६ ॥

46. tapasvibhyo' dhiko yogī
jñānibhyo' pi mato' dhikaḥ
karmibhyaś cādhiko yogī
tasmād yogī bhavārjuna

तपस्विभ्य: -than ascetics, अधिक: - superior, योगी- the Yogi, ज्ञानिभ्य: -than the wise, अपि-even, मत: -thought, अधिक: - superior, कर्मिभ्य: - than the man of action, च-and, अधिक: -superior, योगी-Yogi, तस्मात्- therefore, योगी-a Yogi, भव-be, अर्जुन- O Arjuna.

46. The *Yogi* is thought to be superior to the ascetics, and even superior to men of knowledge (mere studies); he is also superior to men of action; therefore, (you strive to) be a *Yogi* O Arjuna.

In order to bring out the importance of meditation among the various practices in the science of spiritual development, Lord Krishna is making here a truly tabulated list of the various types of seekers, indicating the greatest of the whole lot. Nobler than those who practise thoughtless and dull-witted physical self-denials (*tapasvins)* is the meditator. Nobler than those who vigorously read the scriptures and try to learn and remember their declarations (*gyanis*) is the *Yogi (*meditator)

There are others who strive towards the same bright Peak of Perfection, treading along the path of selfless work (*karmis*) undertaken in the world outside in a spirit of Yagna*, and who perform worship (*upasana)* in a spirit of selfless dedication. These ritualists, both in the secular and in the sacred fields of activities, believe that they can reach the Infinite Bliss through these very activities.

Krishna here concludes that a silent and quiet meditator who struggles hard to withdraw himself from his own false identifications with his body, mind, and intellect through constant and consistent contemplation upon the nature of the Self, is ever the best.

Thus, comparing a meditator with a man of utter self-denials, deep students of the scriptures, and ritualists, Krishna concludes his observation that a meditator alone is the best among the whole lot, standing nearest to Truth, and '*therefore, you be a Yogi (meditator), O Arjuna.*'

There are different types of meditators, each meditating upon a different point of contemplation. Who among them is then the best, and the greatest meditator ? Listen....

योगिनामपि सर्वेषां मद्गतेनान्तरात्मना ।
श्रद्धावान् भजते यो मां स मे युक्ततमो मत: ॥ ४७ ॥

---

* See Chapter IV. 24-30.

47. yoginām api saraveṣām
madgatenā' ntarātmanā
śrāddhāvān bhajate yo mām
sa me yuktatamo mataḥ

योगिनाम्-of Yogis, अपि-even, सर्वेषाम्-of all, मद्गतेन-merged in Me, अन्तरात्मना-with inner-self, श्रद्धावान् -endued with faith, भजते-worships, यः -who, माम् -me, सः - he, मे - by Me, युक्ततम् - most devout, मतः - is deemed.

47. And among all *Yogis,* he who, full of faith, with his innerself merged in Me, worships Me, he is, according to Me, the most devout.

If the previous stanza gives us a relative estimate of the different paths in spirituality and finally declares that meditation is the best among the lot, the stanza under review explains who exactly is the best among all the meditators. Meditation is, in the beginning at least, a deliberate act by which the seeker strives to keep his thoughts channelised into one predetermined line of thinking; and this is maintained by disallowing the mind running into dissimilar thoughtchannels. Meditation, therefore, must, of necessity, start with an effort on the part of the meditator to fix his mind upon some object of contemplation or other.* According to the nature of the object of contemplation chosen, and according to the nature of the persuasions adopted in curtailing the mind from its mad roamings, the art of meditation can be classified under different types.

Thus we have, in the tradition of our practices, meditations prescribed upon a symbol, on a God-principle with a form, on the teacher, on the *kundalini,* on any of the great elements, or on a chosen text in the scripture. Accordingly, the practitioners may be considered as followers of different kinds of meditation. The Singer of the Geeta is trying to indicate herein who exactly is to be considered as the best and the most successful meditator among the above-mentioned types.

In this concluding stanza of the chapter, the Lord insists that, of all the meditators, he who *with his inner-self (mind-and intellect) merged in the Self and with sraddha, devotes himself to the Self,* is the most firm and steadfast meditator. The pregnant suggestions contained in this stanza can fill volumes inasmuch as it is a summary of the entire *Yoga Sastra.* Naturally therefore, Lord Krishna dedicates the entire length of the next chapter as an *annotation* to this *mantra*-like stanza.

* Read Swamiji's *Meditation and Life.*

For the purpose of our understanding this chapter, it is sufficient, for the time being, if we gather from this stanza that the essence of meditation is not so much in our attempts at integrating the mind as in the ultimate merging of the inner equipment (*antah karana)* and getting it completely sublimated in the final experience of the Self. And that it can be done only by one who does proper *bhajan* upon the Self with all *sraddha* is the truth-declaration made with loving insistence here by the Eternal Lover of the Gopis.

The term *bhajan* has come to gather upon itself such a lot of adventitious superstitions that the word, as it is understood today, means elaborate rituals which, almost always, mean nothing to the priest who performs them nor to the devoted who are the onlookers. Sometimes it means a lot of singing with accompaniments and an entire crowd roaring their way towards an emotional ecstasy, often ending in hysteria and exhaustion; and very rarely do they gain even a vague experience of the spiritual thrill. In the Vedantic textbooks, *bhajan* is the attempt of the ego to pour out itself in an act of devoted dedication towards the Principle of Reality whereby it successfully invokes the experience that lies beyond the noisy shores of the mind-intellect. One who does this invocation *(bhajan)* of the Self, and naturaly gets himself merged in that awakening, is declared here by the teacher in the Geeta as belonging to the highest type of meditation.

It is quite self-evident to every student of Vedanta that such a meditator comes to transcend all his identifications with the false matter-envelopments and becomes, through the experience of his Real Nature, the very Self. Yet the mouthpiece of renascent Hinduism, Lord Krishna, in his modesty and reverence for the tradition in our culture, attributes his statement to his own personal opinion in this stanza.

ॐ तत्सदिति श्रीमद्भगवद्गीतासूपनिषत्सु ब्रह्मविद्यायां योगशास्त्रे
श्रीकृष्णार्जुनसंवादे ध्यानयोगो नाम षष्ठोऽध्याय:

Om Tat Sat iti srimad bhagavadgitasūpaniṣatsu
brahmavidyāyām yogaśāstre sri kṛṣṇārjuna
samvāde Dhyanāyogo nāma ṣaṣṭho' dhyāyaḥ

Thus, in the Upanishads of the glorious Bhagawad Geeta, in the Science of the Eternal, in the scripture of Yoga, in the dialogue between Sri Krishna and Arjuna, the sixth discourse ends entitled: THE YOGA OF MEDITATION.

Nowhere else in the entire extent of the voluminous spiritual literature that we have in the *Upanishads,* the *Brahmasutra,* and the *Geeta (Prasthana-traya)* can we find such a wealth of details, explaining not only the technique of meditation but also the possible pitfalls and how to avoid them successfully, as we have them so clearly and vividly explained here. No scripture fails to hint at the Path of Meditation as truly the way to reach the highest possibilities in life, and yet, nowhere have we, among our reported and compiled heritage of sacred books, such a vivid discussion of the entire path. To a true seeker, indeed, a thorough study of the sixth chapter is ample direction and guidance to reach the highest through meditation. It is therefore but proper that this chapter is put under the title: *'The Yoga of Meditation'.*

For other portions of the *sankalpa vakya,* see the same terms explained at the close of Chapters I and II.